Reviews of
<u>Caveman Gumbo--Collected Wit and Wisdom</u>

In these troubled times, this book will give you many smiles and laughs. I love to pick this book up and turn to any page to chase the blues away.

This collection of wit and aphoristic wisdom is a contemporary Tao Te Ching. Read it cover to cover, or cherry pick the sections that speak to you right now. You will not be disappointed, either way.

I can't pick it up without laughing out loud

…one of those books you don't want to put down. On the other hand, you don't want to finish it either…

Everything from quotes from our world's brightest minds to sayings on bumper stickers. Hilarious, illuminating, and truthful…Shows that life is simpler than we make it out to be.

Had I known all of the great info in the book my life would have been better.

This book is hilarious. It had us all weeping at the dinner table last night. I'm ordering five of them for Hostess gifts, or just to make friends feel better.

The book is filled with humor, wisdom, and reminders of human decency.

Funny and thoughtful. What more could you want?

CAVEMAN POTLUCK

COLLECTED WIT AND WISDOM VOL II

WILL BRADY
DAVE CROSS

BEACHTOWN PUBLICATIONS
LAGUNA BEACH CALIFORNIA

Copyright 2019 Dave Cross, Will Brady
ISBN# 978-0-578-49085-4

POB 4321 Laguna Beach CA 92652

PREFACE

Willy:

I guess this volume looks like a reference book (categories of quotes in alphabetical order, yawn) but it's more than that. It's also a sort-of novel with 1000 authors. A chorus of better angels offering up their observations, humorous and otherwise, about living in this world. The reader is the main character with all his brothers and sisters commenting on each facet of life: parents, kids, money, politics, spirit, growing old, attitude. I love that men and women throughout history have found the right words to express their good thoughts in easily digested small bites. Experience, humor, imagination, sarcasm, wonder, irony, logic, nonsense...flavors of life...their memorable ideas helping me see things in perspective.

Dave Cross and I are ancient buddies and have had somewhat parallel lives; 24/7 teachers and players of music, and each of our tribes throwing somewhat notorious BBQ/pot luck parties. This collection is a pot luck of ideas. All the basic recipes, each with a little unique zing. The bright side, I like to think.

Dave:

There is much wisdom and humor, as well as much bullshit, in the world. What you have in *Caveman Gumbo* and *Caveman Potluck* is this massive accumulation of truth, humor and bullshit generated over the ages filtered through Will Brady and Dave Cross. 70+ years on the planet in many guises and absurd situations, as well as deeply satisfying loves and works--and still plugging along. Gratitude, attitude (still working on the humility and compassion part); frugality always a given.

Caveman Gumbo momentum made *Caveman Potluck* inevitable.

My great good fortune to have connected with Willy on these 'weighty tomes'. After many music collaborations over the years, BBQ events, family connections, gigs, the inspiration to publish this collection seems a gesture towards a shared love for our "better angels," as Willy calls it. Special thanks to family and friends, whose soulful additions and insights brought magic to the project. In particular, Tom Newbill, the oldest person we know.

CONTENTS

ADVERTISING

Advertising is the art of convincing people to spend money they don't have for something they don't need. (Will Rogers)

Advertising--a judicious mixture of flattery and threats. (Northrup Frye)

Creative without strategy is called 'art.' Creative with strategy is called 'advertising.' (Jef I. Richards, Professor and Chair of the Department of Advertising, Michigan State University)

Many a small thing has been made large by the right kind of advertising. (Mark Twain)

The true axis of evil in America is the brilliance of our marketing combined with the stupidity of our people. (Bill Maher)

You really want to get a headache? Try to understand internet advertising. (Barry Diller)

As I see it, fast food outfits have targeted small children with their advertising in a very effective way. You know, it's clowns and kid's toys and bright colors and things like that. (Anthony Bourdain)

Advertising works most effectively when it's in line with what people are already trying to do. And people are trying to communicate in a certain way on Facebook-- they share information with their friends, they learn about what their friends are doing--so there's really a whole new opportunity for a new type of advertising model within that. (Mark Zuckerberg)

The advertising world had spacemen in it before spacemen existed. (Fred Allen)

Many billboards and magazine ads have resorted to showing isolated body parts rather than full-body portraits of models using or wearing products. This style of photography, known in the industry as abstract representation, allows the viewer to see himself in the advertisement, rather than the model. (Douglas Rushkoff)

I still remember the five points of salesmanship: attention, interest, conviction, desire and close. (Annette Benning, American actress)

All papers that matter live off their advertisements, and the advertisers exercise an indirect censorship over news. (George Orwell)

It is the advertiser who provides the newspaper for the subscriber. It is not to be disputed, that the publisher of a newspaper in this country, without a very exhaustive advertising support, would receive less reward for his labor than the humblest mechanic. (Alexander Hamilton, 1755-1804)

'Iggy' was my dog--he was named after Iggy Pop--and 'Azalea' is the street where I grew up. Together they have the right amount of syllables to make the perfect name. (Iggy Azalea)

I have always believed that writing advertisements is the second most profitable form of writing. The first, of course, is ransom notes. (Phil Dusenberry, 1936-2007, American advertising executive)

It is really not so repulsive to see the poor asking for money as to see the rich asking for more money. And advertisement is the rich asking for more money. (Gilbert K. Chesterton)

The rich philistinism emanating from advertisements is due not to their exaggerating (or inventing) the glory of this or that serviceable article but to suggesting that the acme of human happiness is purchasable and that it's purchase somehow ennobles the purchaser. (Vladimir Nabokov, 1899-1977, Russian novelist)

Courteous treatment will make a customer a walking advertisement. (James Cash "J.C." Penney)

I have discovered the most exciting, the most arduous literary form of all, the most difficult to master, the most pregnant in curious possibilities. I mean the advertisement. It is far easier to write ten possibly effective Sonnets, good enough to take in the not too inquiring critic, than one effective advertisement that will take in a few thousand of the uncritical buying public.
 (Aldous Huxley, 1894-1963, English writer)

What is the difference between unethical and ethical advertising? Unethical advertising uses falsehoods to deceive the public; ethical advertising uses truth to deceive the public. (Vilhjalmur Stefansson)

Some people have a taboo about doing advertising in the States. You know, where they kind of make their bread and butter. But to me, that's crazy. (Ice Cube)

In our factory, we make lipstick. In our advertising, we sell hope. (Peter Nivio Zarienga)

It is pretty obvious that the debasement of the human mind caused by a constant flow of fraudulent advertising is no trivial thing. There is more than one way to conquer a country. (Raymond Chandler, 1888-1959, American & British novelist)

Advertising is the greatest art form of the 20th century. (Marshall McLuhan, 1911-1980, Canadian professor)

You can tell the ideals of a nation by its advertising. (Norman Douglas)

Until the rise of American advertising, it never occurred to anyone anywhere in the world that the teenager was a captive in a hostile world of adults. (Gore Vidal)

Censorship is advertising paid by the government. (Federico Fellini)

I've done a number of Super Bowl ads. And that is the best advertising of the year. That is when people realize they're going to be compared directly against other ads. (Jerry Seinfeld)

I saw a subliminal advertising executive, but only for a second. (Steven Wright)

I know that campaigns can seem small, and even silly. Trivial things become big distractions. Serious issues become sound bites. And the truth gets buried under an avalanche of money and advertising. If you're sick of hearing me approve this message, believe me--so am I. (Barack Obama)

If advertisers spent the same amount of money on improving their products as they do on advertising, then they wouldn't have to advertise them. (Will Rogers)

Advertising treats all products with the reverence and the seriousness due to sacraments. (Thomas Merton)

Advertising ministers to the spiritual side of trade. It is great power that has been entrusted to your keeping which charges you with the high responsibility of inspiring and ennobling the commercial world. It is all part of the greater work of the regeneration and redemption of mankind. (Calvin Coolidge, POTUS 1923-1929)

Chess is as elaborate a waste of human intelligence as you can find outside an advertising agency. (Raymond Chandler)

When it comes to scaring the bourgeoisie into showing up at the polls, nothing works better than negative advertising. (Tucker Carlson)

The error that we tend to make is that we think that women's magazines are what editors want and what their readers want--and thus are social indicators--when, in fact, they are what advertisers want. They're just advertising indicators. (Gloria Steinem)

The only prejudice I've found anywhere in TV is in some advertising agencies, and there isn't so much prejudice as just fear. (Nat King Cole)

When governments rely increasingly on sophisticated public relations agencies, public debate disappears and is replaced by competing propaganda campaigns, with all the accompanying deceits. Advertising isn't about truth or fairness or rationality, but about mobilizing deeper and more primitive layers of the human mind.
  (Brian Eno)

The future of advertising is the Internet. (Bill Gates)

The distance between Don Quixote and the petty bourgeois victim of advertising is not so great as romanticism would have us believe. (Rene Girard)

Advertising is an environmental striptease for a world of abundance. (Marshall McLuhan)

Every night I watch the nightly news. It's funded by the pharmaceutical companies. Virtually every ad is a drug ad. They get their say every night on the nightly news through advertising. (Michael Moore)

ANIMALS

Women and cats will do as they please, and men and dogs should relax and get used to the idea. (Robert A. Heinlein)

A cat does furnish a room. Like a graceful vase, a cat, even when motionless, seems to flow. (George F. Will)

No matter how much cats fight, there always seems to be plenty of kittens. (Abraham Lincoln)

Man is the only animal that is never satisfied. (Henry George)

Mockingbirds don't do one thing but make music for us to enjoy. They don't eat up people's gardens, don't nest in corncribs, they don't do one thing but sing their hearts out for us. That's why it's a sin to kill a mockingbird.
  (Harper Lee, author of *To Kill a Mockingbird,* 1960*)*

When you look into the eyes of an animal you've rescued, you can't help but fall in love. (Paul Shaffer)

A man who carries a cat by the tail learns something he can learn in no other way. (Mark Twain)

I have a memory like an elephant. I remember every elephant I've ever met. (Herb Caen, *San Francisco Chronicle* journalist)

What a dog I got--his favorite bone is in my arm.
  (Rodney Dangerfield)

The clever cat eats cheese and breathes down rat holes with baited breath. (W.C. Fields)

Time's fun when you're having flies. (Kermit the frog)

7

Just as our ancient ancestors drew animals on cave walls and carved animals from wood and bone, we decorate our homes with animal prints and motifs, give our children stuffed animals to clutch, cartoon animals to watch, animal stories to read. (Diane Ackerman, contemporary American poet, essayist)

No need to teach an eagle to fly. (Greek proverb)

A boy can learn a lot from a dog: obedience, loyalty, and the importance of turning around three times before lying down. (Robert Benchley)

I worked in a pet store and people would ask how big I would get. (Rodney Dangerfield)

It is through this mysterious power that we too have our being, and we therefore yield to our neighbors, even to our animal neighbors, the same right as ourselves to inhabit this vast land. (Sitting Bull)

A tiger does not have to proclaim its tigritude. (Nigerian proverb)

Clouseau: Does yer dawg bite?
Inn Keeper: No.
Clouseau: Nice Doggy. (Bends down to pet a dachshund—it snarls and bites him) I thought you said yer dawg did not bite!
Inn Keeper: Zat…is not my dog! (*The Pink Panther*, 1963)

To a teacher of languages there comes a time when the world is but a place of many words and man appears a mere talking animal not much more wonderful than a parrot. (Joseph Conrad)

Cats don't catch mice to please God.

I've never met an animal I didn't like, and I can't say the same thing about people. (Doris Day)

We are certainly in a common class with the beasts; every action of animal life is concerned with seeking bodily pleasure and avoiding pain. (Saint Augustine)

A black cat crossing your path signifies that the animal is going somewhere. (Groucho Marx)

If I have any beliefs about immortality, it is that certain dogs I have known will go to heaven, and very, very few persons. (James Thurber)

I ask people why they have deer heads on their walls. They always say because it's such a beautiful animal. There you go. I think my mother is attractive, but I have photographs of her. (Ellen DeGeneres)

A man can live and be healthy without killing animals for food; therefore, if he eats meat, he participates in taking animal life merely for the sake of his appetite. (Leo Tolstoy)

For many people who are so lost in their minds, so much involved in their thought processes, the only moments they have when they are not trapped in that way is when they are relating to their animal, their pet. (Eckhart Tolle)

There's nothing funnier than the human animal. (Walt Disney)

When I was 7 and went to the zoo with my second-grade class, I saw chimpanzee eyes for the first time--the eyes of an unhappy animal, all alone, locked in a bare, concrete-floored, iron-barred cage in one of the nastier, old-fashioned zoos. I remember looking at the chimp, then looking away. (Octavia E. Butler, 1947-2006, African-American science-fiction writer)

I'm suspicious of people who don't like dogs, but I trust a dog when it doesn't like a person. (Bill Murray)

When there are dogs and music, people have a good time. (Emmylou Harris)

I'd rather be cleaning a stall than be shopping at the mall. (T-shirt)

Dogs do not ruin their sleep worrying about how to keep the objects they have, and to obtain the objects they have not. There is nothing of value they have to bequeath except their love and their faith. (Eugene O'Neill)

Cats seem to go on the principal that it never does any harm to ask for what you want. (Joseph Wood)

The reason I love my dog so much is because when I come home, he's the only one in the world who treats me like I'm the Beatles. (Bill Maher)

I find reptiles interesting, but the thing about reptiles is that they really just wanna be left alone, and I understand them. It's, 'Don't pick me up, stop holding me, don't look at me, just leave me alone.' I have to admit, sometimes I feel like that. (Nicholas Cage)

There are two means of refuge from the miseries of life: music and cats. (Albert Schweitzer)

Dachshund: A half-a-dog high and a dog-and-a-half long. (H. L. Mencken)

An ostrich's eye is bigger than its brain.

I think dogs are the most amazing creatures; they give unconditional love. For me they are role models for being alive. (Gilda Radner)

God loved the birds and invented trees. Man loved the birds and invented cages. (Jacques Deval)

I called a discount exterminator. A guy came by with a rolled-up magazine. (Wil Shriner)

Many of the qualities that come so effortlessly to dogs—loyalty, devotion, selflessness, unflagging optimism, unqualified love—can be elusive to humans. (John Grogan)

I believe cats to be spirits come to earth. A cat, I am sure, could walk on a cloud without coming through. (Jules Verne)

As far as I can recall, the initial shiver of inspiration [for Lolita] was somehow prompted by a newspaper story about an ape in the Jardin des Plantes, who, after months of coaxing by a scientist, produced the first drawing ever charcoaled by an animal. This sketch showed the bars of the poor creature's cage. (Vladimir Nabokov)

I make up different names for my cat all the time…Flapjack, Bowtie, Popcorn. But he's really, "Hey you, cat." (Christopher Walken)

The fox pissed in the sea and said: This is mine!

No one in the world needs a mink coat but a mink. (Dr. Murray Banks, clinical psychologist)

11

The dog was created especially for children. He is the god of frolic. (Henry Ward Beecher)

Always carry a flagon of whiskey in case of snakebite and furthermore always carry a small snake. (W. C. Fields)

Many animals probably need glasses, but nobody knows it.

Dogs don't rationalize. They don't hold anything against a person. Dogs don't see the outside of a human but the inside. (Cesar Millan)

Dogs have boundless enthusiasm but no sense of shame. I should have a dog as a life coach. (Moby)

Having a bunch of cats around is good. If you're feeling bad, you just look at the cats, you'll feel better because they know that everything is just as it is. There's nothing to get excited about. They just know. (Charles Bukowski)

One dog barks at something, the rest bark at him.
  (Chinese proverb)

Rabbits never cheat or lie
Rabbits only multiply
  (Bob Hare, beat poet, coffeehouse owner, early 60's)

Only mad dogs and Englishmen go out in the noonday sun. (Indian proverb)

One farmer says to me, "You cannot live on vegetable food solely, for it furnishes nothing to make the bones with," and so he religiously devotes a part of his day to supplying himself with the raw material of bones, walking all the while he talks behind his oxen, which, with vegetable-made bones, jerk him and his lumbering plow along in spite of every obstacle. (Henry David Thoreau)

If you don't want your dog to have bad breath, do what I do: Pour a little Lavoris in the toilet. (Jay Leno)

It's easy to trust a cat once you put the cream out of reach. (Argentine proverb)

"Meow" means "Woof" in cat. (George Carlin)

My neighbor has two dogs. One of them says to the other, "Woof." The other replies, "Moo." The first dog is perplexed. "Moo? Why did you say Moo?" "I'm trying to learn a foreign language." (Morey Amsterdam)

Cat's urine glows under a black light.

People who keep dogs are cowards who haven't got the guts to bite people themselves. (August Strindberg, 1849-1912, Swedish writer)

Among animals, one has a sense of humor. (Marianne Moore)

Owners of dogs will have noticed that, if you provide them with food and water and shelter and affection, they will think you are God. Whereas owners of cats are compelled to realize that, if you provide them with food and water and shelter and affection, they draw the conclusion that they are God. (Christopher Hitchens)

Advice for the concerned owner of a 12-year-old, ailing dog: Be your dog. Seriously. Dogs live in the moment. Take your cue from your dog. Who, by the way, will be happier when he feels your Zen. (Vivian Goo, physical therapist)

He is your friend, your partner, your defender, your dog. You are his life, his love, his leader. He will be yours, faithful and true, to the last beat of his heart. You owe it to him to be worthy of that devotion.

Four legs good, two legs bad. (George Orwell)

ARTS

You use a glass mirror to see your face; you use works of art to see your soul. (George Bernard Shaw)

Some painters transform the sun into a yellow spot, others transform a yellow spot into the sun. (Pablo Picasso)

I'm a songwriter. Everything affects me. (Taylor Swift)

Art is the only way to run away without leaving home. (Twyla Tharp)

The Beatles saved the world from boredom. (George Harrison)

A good guitarist will play on one string. (South American proverb)

Right from the beginning, I always strived to capture everything I saw as completely as possible. (Norman Rockwell)

Melody is king. (Ron Eschete, jazz guitarist)

Melody is king, and don't you ever forget it. Lyrics appear to be out front, but they're not; they're just an accompanying factor. If they're good, you're really in good shape. (Quincy Jones)

Immature poets imitate; mature poets steal; bad poets deface what they take, and good poets make it into something better, or at least something different. (T.S. Elliot)

The gateway to freedom was somewhere close to New Orleans where most Africans were sorted through and

15

sold. I had driven through New Orleans on tour and I'd been told my great grandfather had lived way back up in the woods among the evergreens in a log cabin. I revived the era with a song about a colored boy named Johnny B. Goode. My first thought was to make his life follow as my own had come along, but I thought it would seem biased to white fans to say 'colored boy' and changed it to 'country boy'. (Chuck Berry)

To be an author is about the most thankless job there is. (Soren Kierkegaard)

Three recently deceased men arrive at St. Peter's Pearly Gates to qualify for admission into Heaven.
St. Peter. "Tell me what you've earned and how much you've donated to charity."
First candidate: "In my later years I made over $120,000 annually and always donated at least 10% to charity."
St Peter. "You're in; welcome to Heaven."
Second candidate: "I've been incredibly fortunate; at the end of my life I was worth over 20 million dollars and in my will left 50% to charity."
St Peter. "Congratulations and welcome to Heaven."
Third candidate: "Well, last year I earned $8,000…"
St Peter. "Really! What instrument do you play?"

It wasn't until I gave up on being an artist that I realized that work and purpose could be connected. (Gabe Cross)

I'd rather regret the things I've done than regret the things I haven't done. (Lucille Ball)

Comedy may be big business but it isn't pretty. (Steve Martin)

Jazz is the big brother of the blues. If a guy's playing blues like we play, he's in high school. When he starts

16

playing jazz it's like going on to college, to a school of higher learning. (B. B. King)

There is not one female comic who was beautiful as a little girl. (Joan Rivers)

When I hear music, I fear no danger. I am invulnerable. I see no foe. I am related to the earliest times, and to the latest. (Henry David Thoreau)

Hard Day's Night was one of those great films that will never happen again to anyone in their lifetime. The advanced sales on the album...UA was in profit before we'd even finished shooting. (Richard Lester, American film director based in Britain, best known for his work with the Beatles in the 1960s)

All in all it was my intention to hold both the black and the white clientele by voicing the different kinds of songs in their customary tongues. (Chuck Berry)

How *I Love Lucy* was born? We decided that instead of divorce lawyers profiting from our mistakes, we'd profit from them. (Lucille Ball)

Paintings! They're like TV, but they don't move. (A. J. Jacobs, American journalist, author, and lecturer)

Excuse my enthusiasm, or rather madness, for I am really drunk with intellectual vision whenever I take a pencil or graver into my hand. (William Blake)

The difference between a good artist and a bad one is: the bad artist seems to copy a great deal, the good one really does. (William Blake)

The arts are not a way to make a living. They are a very human way of making life more bearable. Practicing an

17

art, no matter how well or badly, is a way to make your soul grow, for heaven's sake. (Kurt Vonnegut)

I love musicians. I think artists are the most amazing people because they are constantly creating beauty for the world. With all the crazy stuff going on in the world, there's artists reminding us of our humanity and reminding us of our heart and soul and what really matters. (Christie Brinkley)

All religions, arts and sciences are branches of the same tree. (Albert Einstein)

Culture is the arts elevated to a set of beliefs. (Thomas Wolfe)

I like chords that are very lush with all the lush parts taken out. (Carla Bley)

Only one thing is impossible for God: To find any sense in any copyright law on the planet. (Mark Twain)

The more I think about it, the more I realize there is nothing more artistic than to love others. (Vincent van Gogh)

The Greek Muse in charge of music is Calliope. (Dion Wright)

Surely you do not think that criticism is the answer to a sum. The richer the work of art the more diverse are the interpretations. There is not one answer only, but many answers. I pity that book on which critics all agree. It must be a very obvious and shallow production. (Oscar Wilde)

I see music in colors. I love music that's black, pink, purple or red, but hate music that's green, yellow or brown. (Charli XCX, English singer, songwriter, music video director)

The best time to plan a book is while you're doing the dishes. (Agatha Christie)

At this time the fashion is to bring something to jazz that I reject. They speak of freedom. But one has no right, under pretext of freeing yourself, to be illogical and incoherent by getting rid of structure and simply piling a lot of notes one on top of the other. There's no beat anymore. You can't keep time with your foot. I believe that what is happening to jazz with people like Ornette Coleman, for instance, is bad. There's a new idea that consists in destroying everything and find what's shocking and unexpected; whereas jazz must first of all tell a story that anyone can understand. (Thelonious Monk)

If you come on a band tense, you're going to play tense. If you come a little bit foolish, act just a little bit foolish, and let yourself go, better ideas will come. (Thelonious Monk)

Ever since I've ever heard music, I thought it should be very clean, very precise--as clean as possible, anyway, and more or less tuned to people. Something they could understand, something that was beautiful, you know?
  (Thelonious Monk)

I put quite a bit of study into the horn, that's true. In fact, the neighbors threatened to ask my mother to move once, you know. (Charlie Parker)

When you do anything too long, you either wear it out or lose interest. (Miles Davis)

Art is not a handicraft, it is the transmission of feeling the artist has experienced. (Leo Tolstoy)

Nobody, I think, ought to read poetry, or look at pictures or statues, who cannot find a great deal more in them than the poet or artist has actually expressed. Their highest merit is suggestiveness. (Nathaniel Hawthorne)

I say, play your own way. Don't play what the public wants. You play what you want and let the public pick up on what you're doing; even if it does take them fifteen, twenty years. (Thelonious Monk)

I am an artist. Art has no color and no sex. (Whoopi Goldberg)

You can write 16 plays and not make as much money as you did doing one movie. (Sam Shepard, American actor, playwright, author, screenwriter)

Writing is rewriting. (August Wilson)

Most comedy is based on getting a laugh at someone else's expense. And I find that that's just a form of bullying in a major way. So I want to be an example that you can be funny and be kind, and make people laugh without hurting somebody else's feelings. (Ellen DeGeneres)

Amateurs hope. Professionals work. (Garson Kanin)

I've been doing a lot of abstract painting lately. Extremely abstract. No brush, no paint, no canvas, I just think about it. (Steven Wright)

Music is shorthand for emotion. Emotions, which let themselves be described in words with such difficulty, are directly conveyed to man in music, and in that is its power and significance. (Leo Tolstoy)

I don't consider myself a musician who has achieved perfection and can't develop any further. But I compose my pieces with a formula that I created myself. Take a musician like John Coltrane. He is a perfect musician, who can give expression to all the possibilities of his instrument. But he seems to have difficulty expressing original ideas on it. That is why he keeps looking for ideas in exotic places. At least I don't have that problem, because, like I say, I find my inspiration in myself.
  (Thelonious Monk)

For me, visuals are as important as the music. I just love escapism and giving people something to escape to. To me, that's what art is. (Iggy Azalea, Australian rapper, singer, songwriter, and model)

Not every artist is a role model. (Iggy Azalea)

I love watching people listen. And on film often some of the best moments, if you think about favorite moments on film, often the person isn't even talking. (Annette Benning, American actress)

How difficult it is to be simple. (Irving Stone, American writer)

The reason some portraits don't look true to life is that some people make no effort to resemble their pictures.
  (Salvador Dali)

I always say that I write for the same people that Picasso painted for. I think he painted for himself. (August Wilson, American playwright, two Pulitzer Prizes for drama)

Humor disarms people. They don't feel threatened.
(Bette Midler)

One should not become an artist because he can, but
because he must. It is only for those who would be
miserable without it. (Irving Stone)

The good, the admirable reader identifies himself not
with the boy or the girl in the book, but with the mind that
conceived and composed that book. (Vladimir Nabokov)

Although knowledge of structure is helpful, real creativity
comes from leaps of faith in which you jump to
something illogical. But those leaps form the memorable
moments in movies and plays. (Francis Ford Coppola)

Art lifts man from his personal life into the universal life.
(Leo Tolstoy)

Avant-garde means never having to say you're sorry.
(Marc Ribot, American guitarist and composer)

The older I get, the more acutely I am aware that the
vast majority of what is written remains unread. (Jhumpa
Lahiri, American-Indian author)

You get ideas from daydreaming. You get ideas from
being bored. You get ideas all the time. The only
difference between writers and other people is we notice
when we're doing it. (Neil Gaiman, English author)

The freelance writer is a man who is paid per piece or
per word or perhaps. (Robert Benchley, American
humorist, newspaper columnist and film actor)

Bass guitar is the engine of the band. (Suzi Quatro,
American rock singer-songwriter, multi-instrumentalist
and actress)

An actor's a guy who, if you ain't talking about him, he ain't listening. (Marlon Brando)

If there's a book you really want to read, but it hasn't been written yet, then you must write it. (Toni Morrison, American novelist, essayist, editor, teacher, and professor emeritus at Princeton University)

Painting is a faith, and it imposes the duty to disregard public opinion. (Vincent van Gogh)

Theater is a series of insurmountable obstacles on a road to imminent disaster. (Tom Stoppard)

You never really understand a person until you consider things from his point of view--until you climb into his skin and walk around in it. (Harper Lee, author of *To Kill a Mockingbird*)

I envy people who can just look at a sunset. I wonder how you can shoot it. (Dustin Hoffman)

There's no one way to be creative. Any old way will work. (Ray Bradbury)

Everything I wrote about wasn't about me, but about the people listening. (Chuck Berry)

Color is so intuitive. (Milton Glaser)

You can't show a gun in the first act and not have it go off by the third act. (George Bernard Shaw)

The Clark Fork Two-Step:
    Step one: both feet in the air.
    Step two: both feet on the floor.
    Repeat.
  (Dave Cross, from a gig in Clark Fork, Idaho)

The actor becomes an emotional athlete. (Al Pacino)

A person is a fool to become a writer. His only compensation is absolute freedom. (Roald Dahl)

Genius is the recovery of childhood at will. (Arthur Rimbaud)

Movie acting suits me because I only need to be good for ninety seconds at a time. (Bill Murray)

One of the things you do when you make a piece of art is you try to make the world you'd rather be in. (Brian Eno, English musician, record producer, and visual artist)

Pop music is aspirin and the blues are vitamins. (Peter Tork, *The Monkees*)

All musicians are subconsciously mathematicians. (Thelonious Monk)

You've got to be a good date for the reader. (Kurt Vonnegut)

The best work that anybody ever writes is the work that is on the verge of embarrassing him, always. (Arthur Miller)

There is love, and there is work, and we have only one heart. (Edgar Degas)

Alfred Hitchcock once told me, when I was analyzing a lot of things about pictures, 'Clint, you must remember, it's only a movie.' (Clint Eastwood)

Art is the antennae of the race. (Ezra Pound)

The artist works at the bottom of a twelve-foot trench with the wind ripping at 300mph across the top, finishes the work, throws it into the air, and starts anew. (Dave Cross)

There is no blue without yellow and without orange. (Vincent van Gogh)

I believe that music is connected by human passions and curiosities rather than by marketing strategies. (Elvis Costello)

Fiction is such a world of freedom, it's wonderful. If you want someone to fly, they can fly. (Alice Walker)

With me, Grand Opera is the berries. (Al Capone)

One day a long time from now you'll cease to care anymore whom you please or what anybody has to say about you. That's when you'll finally produce the work you're capable of. (J. D. Salinger)

I've been imitated so well I've heard people copy my mistakes. (Jimi Hendrix)

I mean, give me a guitar, give me a piano, give me a broom and string, I wouldn't get bored anywhere. (Keith Richards)

The mind of a writer can be a truly terrifying thing: Isolated, neurotic, caffeine-addled, crippled by procrastination, consumed by feelings of panic, self-loathing, and soul-crushing inadequacy. And that's on a good day. (Robert De Niro)

I grew up thinking art was pictures until I got into music and found I was an artist and didn't paint. (Chuck Berry)

The key to the mystery of a great artist is that for reasons unknown, he will give away his energies and his life just to make sure that one note follows another…and leaves us with the feeling that something is right in the world. (Leonard Bernstein)

I dream for a living. (Steven Spielberg)

My stories run up and bite me on the leg. I respond by writing down everything that goes on during the bite. When I finish, the idea lets go and runs off. (Ray Bradbury)

I'm not afraid to write my feelings in a song. (Taylor Swift)

The four stages of a star:
    1 Who's Johnny Starbright?
    2 Get me Johnny Starbright
    3 Get me a young Johnny Starbright
    4 Who's Johnny Starbright?

If you pick up a ukulele, it will make you unbelievably happy. (Bette Midler)

You know as a director what you want, but the film is smarter than you, the film says no, the film says there's something more here. (John Cassavetes)

I have to change. It's like a curse. (Miles Davis)

The most realistic blood I've seen is when Marlon Brando gets beat up in *On the Waterfront*. (George A. Romero, American-Canadian filmmaker, *Night of the Living Dead,* 1968)

Sometimes when I think how good my book can be, I can hardly breathe. (Truman Capote)

I've written some poetry I don't understand myself. (Carl Sandburg)

It was Elvis who really got me hooked on beat music. When I heard *Heartbreak Hotel,* I thought, this is it, (Paul McCartney)

A hunch is creativity trying to tell you something. (Frank Capra)

Groundhog Day is one of the greatest scripts ever written. It didn't even get nominated for an Academy Award. (Bill Murray)

Rock is like a battery that must always go back to the blues to get recharged. (Eric Clapton)

One of my worst fears is people saying my songs all are starting to sound the same. (Taylor Swift)

I've done my bit for motion pictures--I've stopped making them. (Liberace)

If you want to make someone feel emotion, you have to make them let go. Listening to something is an act of surrender. (Brian Eno)

The worst thing you can do is censor yourself as the pencil hits the paper. You must not edit until you get it all on paper. If you can put everything down, stream-of-consciousness, you'll do yourself a service. (Stephan Sondheim)

The poet enjoys the incomparable privilege of being able to be himself and others, as he wishes. (Claude Baudelaire)

I've found that the people who play villains are the nicest people in the world, and people who play heroes are jerks. It's like people who play villains work out all their problems on screen, and then they're just really wonderful people. (Tim Burton)

To draw you must close your eyes and sing. (Pablo Picasso)

When you listen to Ray Charles, there's never any doubt who's voice that is. (Clint Eastwood)

Writing free verse is like playing tennis with the net down. (Robert Frost)

I knew by heart all the dialogue of James Dean's films. I could watch *Rebel without a Cause* a hundred times over. (Elvis Presley)

If you knew how much work went into it, you wouldn't call it genius. (Michelangelo)

What is the best pickup to use on a banjo?...A Ford F-150.

Keith Richards was once asked how he came up with all those amazing guitar riffs. His answer? He just starts playing until he makes the right mistake. In other words, he's optimistic he will create something good by virtue of getting something "wrong." (Mark Stevenson)

The American public does not know poets exist. (James Broughton)

Practice any art, music, singing, dancing, acting, drawing, painting, sculpting, poetry, fiction, essays, reportage, no matter how well or badly, not to get money or fame, but to experience becoming, to find out what's inside you, to make your soul grow. (Kurt Vonnegut)

I really believe there are things nobody would see if I did not photograph them. (Diane Arbus)

Poets are always taking the weather so personally. (J. D. Salinger)

Johnny Otis explaining to Frank Zappa how to get the correct greasy fifties sound from a saxophone: "You point it at the wall, it bounces off the ceiling and you put the mic behind the player, pointed up to catch it."

Impressionism: it is the birth of Light in painting. (Robert Delaunay)

Talent alone won't make you a success. Neither will being in the right place at the right time, unless you are ready. The most important question is: 'Are you ready?' (Johnny Carson)

The people in my songs are all me. (Bob Dylan)

I've had quite a lot of luck with dreams. I've often awoken in the night with a phrase or even a whole song in my head. (Brian Eno)

For me it's all contingent on getting a sound. The sound always suggests what kind of melody it should be. So it's always sound first and then the line afterwards. (Brian Eno)

Let me put it this way: If you're sitting in a movie and you're watching me, and you say, 'Isn't that Michael Caine a wonderful actor?' then I've failed. (Michael Caine)

Imitation is the sincerest form of television. (Fred Allen, actor, comedian, Hollywood Walk of Fame Star)

An abiding tenet of TV is that viewers don't want new shows, they want new shows that remind them of old shows. (Fred Allen)

I know nothing in the world that has as much power as a word. Sometimes I write one, and I look at it until it begins to shine. (Emily Dickenson)

Creativity is allowing yourself to make mistakes. Art is knowing which ones to keep. (Scott Adams, creator of the *Dilbert* comic strip)

The role of a writer is not to say what we all can say, but what we are unable to say. (Anais Nin, 1903-1977, French-American diarist, essayist, novelist)

I don't think writers are sacred, but words are. They deserve respect. If you get the right ones in the right order, you can nudge the world a little or make a poem which children will speak for you when you're dead.
  (Tom Stoppard, Czech-born British playwright and screenwriter)

Exaggerate the essential, leave the obvious vague.
  (Vincent van Gogh)

One of the hippest things Mr. Buchanan taught me was not to play with vibrato in my tone. (Miles Davis about his high school band director)

Motion pictures are the art form of the 20th century, and one of the reasons is the fact that films are a slightly corrupted art form. They fit this century--they combine art and business! (Roger Corman, American director, producer, actor)

Songs are more powerful than books. (Elvis Costello)

The characters Bert and Ernie on *Sesame Street* were named after Bert the cop and Ernie the taxi driver in Frank Capra's *It's a Wonderful Life.*

Opera is a sham art. Large, plain, middle-aged women galumph around posing as pretty young girls singing to portly, plain, middle-aged men posing as handsome young heroes. (Woodrow Wyatt, 1918-1997, British politician, author, journalist, broadcaster)

Talent is like electricity. We don't understand electricity. We use it. (Maya Angelou)

Beautiful things don't ask for attention. (James Thurber)

They used us as an excuse to go mad, the world did, and then blamed it on us. (George Harrison)

Talent is cheap; dedication is expensive. (Irving Stone)

Kids deserve arts, and it's just as important as science, math, history, English, or athletics. (Flea, bass player for The Red Hot Chili Peppers)

Poets, like the blind, can see in the dark. (Jorge Luis Borges)

If I say, 'I am in charge' or even 'I am going to write these kinds of songs,' it never works. I have to listen. (Greg Brown, songwriter)

Before Elvis…there was nothing. (John Lennon)

Nobody has ever written as many enjoyable, fun-to-read crime novels as Agatha Christie. It's all about the storytelling and the pleasure of the reader. She doesn't want to be deep or highbrow. (Sophie Hannah, British poet and novelist)

I saw the angel in the marble and carved until I set him free. (Michelangelo)

My goal is to be one with the music. I just dedicate my whole life to this art. (Jimi Hendrix)

The writers are the stars of every really successful sitcom. (Betty White)

In comic strips, the person on the left always speaks first. (George Carlin)

When I told my friends I was going to be a comedian, they laughed at me. (Carrot Top)

I remember once, years ago, I met Sting, and he told me that he had seen 'Spinal Tap' 50 times. He said, 'Every time I watch it, I don't know whether to laugh or cry.' (Rob Reiner-Director, *This is Spinal Tap,* 1984)

Being a star is an agent's dream, not an actor's. (Robert Duvall)

Insomnia is my greatest inspiration. (Jon Stewart)

I had a band before I did standup. I've always done music. I got known for being funny, and that's how I make my living…and from acting…but I never stopped playing and producing and recording music. (Eddie Murphy)

I do take my work seriously and the way to do that is not to take yourself too seriously. (Alan Rickman-Actor, Professor Severus Snape, *Harry Potter,* 8 movies)

I wrote a few children's books...not on purpose. (Steven Wright)

There is only one true thing: instantly paint what you see. When you've got it, you've got it. When you haven't, you begin again. All the rest is humbug. (Edouard Manet)

If you put it in a beat, it makes it easy to repeat. (Sam Horn)

I won't call my work entertainment. It's exploring. It's asking questions of people, constantly. 'How do you feel? How much do you know? Are you aware of this? Can you cope with this?' A good movie will ask you questions you don't already know the answers to. Why would I want to make a film about something I already understand? (John Cassavetes)

To the best of my knowledge, none of the Beatles can read music. (George Harrison)

I don't like country music, but I don't mean to denigrate those who do. And for the people who like country music, denigrate means 'put down'. (Bob Newhart)

I paint flowers so they do not die. (Frida Kahlo)

Writing, of course, is writing, acting comes from the theater, and cinematography comes from photography. Editing is unique to film. You can see something from different points of view almost simultaneously, and it creates a new experience. (Stanley Kubrick)

Beauty should be edible, or not at all. (Salvador Dali)

Music can name the unnamable and communicate the unknowable. (Leonard Bernstein)

33

I like the opera crowd. I feel tough. (Jerry Seinfeld)

Color is my day-long obsession, joy and torment.
  (Claude Monet, 1840-1926, French painter)

There are no lines in nature, only areas of color, one
against another. (Edouard Manet, 1832-1883, French
painter)

Try to forget what objects you have before you–a tree, a
house, a field, or whatever. Merely think, 'Here is a little
square of blue, here an oblong of pink, here a streak of
yellow,' and paint it just as it looks to you, the exact color
and shape, until it gives you your own impression of the
scene before you. (Claude Monet)

Very rarely do I talk off the top of my head on stage. I'm
not an improv guy. I'm a writer-guy who presents what
he's written. (Steven Wright)

When I was old enough to go to the movies alone, I got
to see *Frankenstein* and *Dracula* on the big screen. I just
fell in love with them. (George A. Romero)

I Got Rhythm really put me on the map. (Ethel Merman)

An artist cannot fail; it is a success to be one. (Charles
Horton Cooley, 1864-1929, American sociologist)

Hitherto the nude has always been represented in poses
that presuppose an audience. But my women are
simple, honest creatures who are concerned with
nothing beyond their physical occupations. It is as if you
were looking through a keyhole. (Edgar Degas)

I love editing. It's one of my favorite parts of filmmaking.
  (Steven Spielberg)

Out of all the guitars in the whole world, the Fender Mustang is my favorite. They're cheap and totally inefficient, and they sound like crap and are very small. (Kurt Cobain, Nirvana, songwriter and guitarist)

The whole problem can be stated quite simply by asking, 'Is there a meaning to music?' My answer would be, 'Yes.' And 'Can you state in so many words what the meaning is?' My answer to that would be, 'No.' (Aaron Copland)

If something is working, don't fix it. Keep going. Go with the glow. (Al Pacino)

When I saw I was under attack from all sides, I knew I was on the right track. (Man Ray)

There is art in in every good sentence. (Friedrich Wilhelm Nietzsche)

One of the most attractive things about writing your autobiography is that you're not dead. (Joseph Barbera, animator, *The Flintstones,* 1960; *The Jetsons,*1962)

When you're a novelist, you're writing a play but acting all the parts, you're controlling the lights and the scenery and the whole business, and it's your show. (Robertson Davies, Canadian novelist, playwright, critic, journalist, and professor)

I'd been studying the microphone for a dozen years, and I suddenly saw what I'd been doing wrong. I'd been singing too loud. One night I was listening to a record of Lester Young, the horn player, and it came to me. Relax, just relax. It's all going to be alright. (Marvin Gaye)

Vagueness is at times an indication of nearness to a perfect truth. (Charles Ives)

People today are still living off the table scraps of the sixties. They are still being passed around---the music and the ideas. (Bob Dylan)

The worst crime is faking it. (Kurt Cobain)

I won't make shorthand films, because I don't want to manipulate audiences into assuming quick, manufactured truths. (John Cassavetes)

Walt Disney and I always said we were two children looking for our inner adults. (Dick Van Dyke)

I used to hear all them musicians playing all them scales and notes and never nothing you could remember. (Miles Davis)

I love it when people come up to me and they say a line, like, you know, "My name is Inigo Montoya. You killed my father. Prepare to die." (Rob Reiner, Director, *The Princess Bride,* 1987*)*

I would rather write or record something great and have it overlooked than do mediocre work and have it be popular. (Patti Smith)

My vocal style I haven't tried to copy from anyone. It just developed until it became the girlish whine it is today. (Robert Plant, lead singer in Led Zeppelin)

The problem with Hollywood studios is that they are cowardly. (Jim Jarmusch, American film director, screenwriter, actor, producer, editor, and composer)

Remember, science fiction's always been the kind of first level of alert to think about things to come. It's easier for an audience to take warnings from sci-fi without feeling that we're preaching to them. Every science fiction movie I have ever seen, any one that's worth its weight in celluloid, warns us about things that ultimately come true. (Steven Spielberg)

Creativity takes courage. (Henri Matisse)

When you feel that you can't fight it, you just go for it. When it comes to the arts, passion should always trump common sense. (Robert De Niro)

ATTITUDE

My mission in life is not merely to survive, but to thrive, and to do so with some passion, some compassion, some humor, and some style. (Maya Angelou)

Don't lower your standards for anything or anybody. (Rihanna)

Not knowing when the dawn will come I open every door. (Emily Dickenson)

No more walls. (Anais Nin)

Wake up,
kick ass,
sleep,
repeat. (T-shirt)

I tried being reasonable. I didn't like it. (Clint Eastwood)

Observe your enemies, for they first find your faults. (Greek proverb)

I don't really care what people think. I just do my own thing. I like being loud and letting people know I'm there. (James Brown, Soul Brother #1)

"Gangsta", to us, didn't have anything to do with Al Capone and stuff like that. It's just about living your life the way you want to live it. And you're not going to let nothing stop you. (Ice Cube)

Everything must be doubted. (Karl Marx)

Sometimes you have to be silent to be heard. (Stanislaw Jerzy Lec, Polish aphorist and poet, 1909-1966)

But Boss, life *is* trouble. Only death is not. To live is to undo your belt and *look* for trouble. (Nikos Kazantzakis, Cretan, author, *Zorba the Greek,* 1946)

If I listen I have advantage, if I speak others have it. (Peruvian proverb)

I have tried to know absolutely nothing about a great many things, and I have succeeded fairly well. (Robert Benchley)

Boasting begins where wisdom stops. (Japanese proverb)

You don't have to rush to do anything. (Robert De Niro)

I have my standards. They're low, but I have them. (Bette Midler)

I have taken more good from alcohol than alcohol has taken from me. (Winston Churchill)

Life would be tragic if it weren't funny. (Stephen Hawking)

Never give up. And never, under any circumstance, face the facts. (Ruth Gordon)

You can learn steps, but you cannot learn how to boogie. (Rosie Perez)

If your daily life seems poor, do not blame it, blame yourself that you are not poet enough to call forth its riches; for the creator, there is no poverty. (Rainer Maria Rilke)

I like to write standing up. (Ernest Hemingway)

Get up and show 'em what you got! (James Brown)

Let all of life be an unfettered howl. (Vladimir Nabokov)

You're going to die. You're going to be dead. It could be 20 years, it could be tomorrow, anytime. So am I. I mean, we're just going to be gone. The world's going to go on without us. All right now. You do your job in the face of that, and how seriously you take yourself you decide for yourself. (Bob Dylan)

Don't wait till you die to go to heaven. (RZA-Wu Tang Clan)

To the extent you treat me badly you expose your sense of inferiority to me.

Pleasure is one of the most important things in life, as important as food or drink. (Irvine Stone)

I've always found it embarrassing to receive awards. (Sam Shepard)

That's the great thing about a tractor. You can't really hear the phone ring. (Jeff Foxworthy)

The flame that burns twice as bright burns half as long. (Lao Tzu, *Te Tao Ching*)

Never put off 'til tomorrow what you can do the day after tomorrow. (Mark Twain)

Never apologize for what you feel.
It's like being sorry for being real. (Lil Wayne)

Coward: one who, in a perilous emergency, thinks with his legs. (Ambrose Bierce)

When illusions are shattered by truth, talent is set free. (Lian Hearn)

Need a reason to be grateful? Check your pulse.

Well done is better than well said. (Benjamin Franklin)

Nobody ever came up with a great idea after a second bottle of water. (Tom Newbill)

Little knowledge generates great pride; the wise are quiet. (Tibetan proverb)

Give me a window and I'll stare out of it. (Alan Rickman, British actor)

Expect anything from anyone. The Devil was once an Angel.

To the mediocre, mediocrity comes out great. (Indian proverb)

A man's first care should be to avoid the reproaches of his own heart, his next to escape the censures of the world. (English proverb)

A speaker of truth has few friends.

Danger can never be overcome without taking risks.

Some men walk through the woods and see no trees. (Mongolian proverb)

Better an also ran than a never ran at all.

I love those who can smile in trouble, who can gather strength from distress, and grow brave by reflection. 'Tis the business of little minds to shrink, but they whose heart is firm, and whose conscience approves their conduct, will pursue their principles unto death. (Leonardo da Vinci)

It is easier to forgive an enemy than to forgive a friend. (William Blake)

People who boast about their I.Q. are losers. (Stephen Hawking)

Mock not the fallen, for slippery is the road ahead of you. (Russian proverb)

Sometimes you win, sometimes you learn. (T-Shirt)

Draw the line, but draw it wide.

Happiness is not a station you arrive at, but a manner of traveling. (Margaret Lee Runbeck)

Faithless is he that says farewell when the road darkens. (J.R.R. Tolkien)

Better to be a tiger for a day than a sheep for a thousand years. (Tibetan proverb)

Explanations and apologies are designed to make the person offering them feel good. If you have to explain yourself, you've already lost.

He who knows that enough is enough will always have enough. (Lao Tzu)

It's not what you look at that matters, it's what you see. (Henry David Thoreau)

Work like you don't need the money. Love like you've never been hurt. Dance like nobody's watching. (Satchel Paige, 1906-1982, American baseball player)

It ain't what they call you, it's what you answer to. (W. C. Fields)

It is a great blessing to be able to laugh at oneself.

Time abides long enough for those who make use of it. (Leonardo da Vinci)

You do something so long it becomes monotonous. You're not inspired to do it so much anymore. It becomes more of a job and less of a passion. (Retired Olympian John Daly explaining why he left the sport of sledding and his return for the 2018 games.)

Yesterday is history, tomorrow is a mystery, today is God's gift, that's why we call it the present. (Joan Rivers)

I found there was only one way to look thin: hang out with fat people. (Rodney Dangerfield)

To self-justify is to self-convince.

The natural desire of good men is knowledge. (Leonardo da Vinci)

I am a nobody, and I have the track record to prove it.

Tomorrow is overrated. (*Jose Cuervo* TV advertisement)

Turn your stumbles into dance steps. (Tom Newbill)

The enlightened person has nothing to prove to himself or others, and thus may always operate from a position of sincerity, with no pretense or posturing. (Sri Ramakrishna)

Superlatives are always perilous.

I'm gonna live like a king for the rest of my life...as long as I die in an hour or two. (*Back To Broke*, Brady, Cross)

The only authentic form of revenge is success. (Frank Sinatra)

If you're going to seek revenge, dig two graves. (Chinese proverb)

The real voyage of discovery consists not in seeking new landscapes, but in having new eyes. (Marcel Proust, French novelist)

Evil, when we are in its power, is not felt as evil but as a necessity, or even a duty. (Simone Weil, French philosopher)

Never pledge to give up a drug when high on it, or a bad habit while indulging it. (Sue Cross)

The noblest pleasure is the joy of understanding. (Leonardo da Vinci)

To be content with oneself is the greatest success imaginable. (Sri Ramakrishna)

I can't relax unless I'm doing two things at once. (Will Brady)

Live your life without attracting attention. (Epicurus, 341-270 B.C , Greek philosopher)

Nothing is enough for the man to whom enough is too little. (Epicurus)

The fool's life is empty of gratitude and full of fears; its course lies wholly toward the future. (Epicurus)

Being happy is knowing how to be content with little. (Epicurus)

We are what we repeatedly do. Excellence, then, is not an act, but a habit. (Aristotle)

No one can make you feel inferior without your consent. (Eleanor Roosevelt)

It is useless to attempt to reason a man out of a thing he was never reasoned into. (Jonathon Swift)

Theology is unnecessary. (Stephen Hawking)

There are few, very few, that will own themselves in a mistake. (Jonathon Swift)

Humility provides everyone, even him who despairs in solitude, with the strongest relationship to his fellow man. (Franz Kafka)

You can't stop talking to yourself—monkey brain—but you can stop listening.

If the ram butts into the hedge, the entangling thorns will prevent both advance and retreat. Recognize and avoid this danger. (*I Ching*)

Life is too short to blend in. (Paris Hilton)

Never let the fear of striking out get in your way. (Babe Ruth)

It's not whether you get knocked down, it's whether you get back up. (Vince Lombardi)

Next in importance to having a good aim is to recognize when to pull the trigger. (David Letterman)

You cannot swim for new horizons until you have courage to lose sight of the shore. (William Faulkner)

When I was a kid and the carnival would come to the shopping center, I'd go down and talk to all the people running the rides. I like that whole lifestyle, moving from town to town in a nomadic existence. (Randy Quaid, American film and television actor)

In for a dime, in for a dollar.

Excellence is never an accident. (H. Jackson Brown)

Sometimes I don't feel like going to work. Sometimes I'm in a bad mood. That's OK. Feelings are not controllable. What we can control is what we do. And that's where freedom lies. (David Reynolds, British historian, Professor)

The more you live, the less you die. (Janis Joplin)

NO FATE (*Terminator 2*)

Avoid unnecessary bullshit. (Miles Davis)

To be a good loser is to learn how to win. (Carl Sandburg)

Smile in the mirror. Do that every morning and you'll start to see a big difference in your life. (Yoko Ono)

All of us every single year, we're a different person. I don't think we're the same person all our lives. (Steven Spielberg)

I'd rather be hated for who I am, than for who I am not. (Kurt Cobain)

It takes as much energy to wish as it does to plan. (Eleanor Roosevelt)

Create like a god; command like a king, work like a slave. (Constantin Brancusi, 1876-1957, Romanian sculptor, painter and photographer)

Humor is but another weapon against the universe. (Mel Brooks)

Dignity does not consist in possessing honors, but in deserving them. (Aristotle)

What you do not want done to yourself, do not do to others. (Confucius)

If my life wasn't funny, it would just be true, and that's unacceptable. (Carrie Fisher)

A Muslim, a Jew, a Christian, and an Atheist all walk into a coffee shop...And they talked, laughed, drank coffee and became good friends. It's not a joke. It's what happens when you're not a jerk. (Tom Newbill)

Never too old, never too bad, never too late, never too sick to start from scratch once again. (Bikram Choudhury, founder of Bikram Yoga)

Fun is good. (Dr. Seuss)

Our greatest glory is not in never failing, but in rising every time we fail. (Confucius)

It's great to be here. It's great to be anywhere. (Keith Richards)

With change comes opportunity. (Sonne & Renate)

Every one of my regrets has produced a song I'm proud of. (Taylor Swift)

ITHEGUY (License Plate)

He is richest who is content with the least, for content is the wealth of nature. (Socrates)

Honor thy error as a hidden intention. (Brian Eno)

Doubt is not below knowledge, but above it. (Alain, French philosopher)

Actions speak louder than words.

Both optimists and pessimists contribute to society. The optimist invents the aeroplane, the pessimist the parachute. (George Bernard Shaw)

I'm not in this world to live up to your expectations and you're not in this world to live up to mine. (Bruce Lee)

When one burns one's bridges, what a very nice fire it makes. (Dylan Thomas)

Never delay kissing a pretty girl or opening a bottle of whiskey. (Ernest Hemingway)

Ambition is a dream with a V8 engine. (Elvis Presley)

Fall forward. Here's what I mean. Reggie Jackson struck out 2,600 times in his career, the most in the history of baseball. But you don't hear about the strikeouts. People remember the home runs. Fall forward. Thomas Edison conducted 1,000 failed experiments. Did you know that? I didn't either...because number 1,001 was the light bulb. Fall forward. Every failed experiment is one step closer to success. (Denzel Washington)

Light is the task where many share the toil. (Homer, *The Odyssey*, 800 B.C.)

Umm, donuts. (Homer, *The Simpsons*, 1989-present)

I think of my body as a side effect of my mind. (Carrie Fisher)

I used to live in a roomful of mirrors; all I could see is me. I take my spirit and I crash my mirrors, now the whole world is here for me to see. (Jimi Hendrix, *Roomful of Mirrors*, 1970)

I'm gonna live 'til I die. (Frank Sinatra)

It's not the having, it's the getting. (Elizabeth Taylor)

Sometimes I go for days without speaking to a soul. I think 'I should make that call' but I put it off. There's something pleasurable about not talking. (Ingmar Bergman)

Love your neighbor as yourself but don't take down the fence. (Carl Sandburg)

Waiting for luck is similar to waiting for death. (Japanese proverb)

Find out who you are and do it on purpose. (Dolly Parton)

AU79REWEL (License Plate)

The Silver Rule---Don't be a dick! (Ry Miller, age 39)

The Platinum Rule---Don't scratch fancy houses. (Simon Miller, age 6)

Don't believe everything you think. (T-Shirt)

Gotta go with what got 'ya here. (P.J. Cochrane)

If you don't go, you'll never know. (Robert De Niro)

BENT CLICHES

Give a man a fish, you feed him for a day. Give a man a poisoned fish, you feed him for the rest of his life. (Aristotle)

I drink therefore I am. (W. C. Fields)

The early bird gets the worm, but the second mouse gets the cheese. (Steven Wright)

(Closing a letter) Onward and Inward, (signature). (Craig Buhler, Honk band, saxophone, clarinet, and flute)

There is an old American saying, 'He who lives in a glass house should not try to kill two birds with one stone.' (Vladimir Nabokov)

No rest for the wacky. (Will Brady)

CRIME

If you attempt to rob a bank you won't have any trouble with rent and food bills for the next 10 years, whether or not you are successful.

A thief passes for a gentleman when stealing has made him rich. (Dutch proverb)

Behind every crime is a story of sadness. (Enrique Pena Nieto, 57th President of Mexico)

Falsehood flies, and the Truth comes limping after it. (Jonathan Swift)

There are four kinds of Homicide: felonious, excusable, justifiable, and praiseworthy. (Ambrose Bierce, American short story writer, journalist, poet, and Civil War veteran)

Punishment is justice for the unjust. (Saint Augustine)

Obedience to lawful authority is the foundation of manly character. (Robert E. Lee)

The successful in this world are the unscrupulous and unjust. (Plato)

Only the weak and defeated are called upon to account for their crimes. (Noam Chomsky)

I submit that an individual who breaks a law that conscience tells him is unjust, and who willingly accepts the penalty of imprisonment in order to arouse the conscience of the community over its injustice, is in reality expressing the highest respect for law. (Martin Luther King, Jr.)

Poverty is the mother of crime. (Marcus Aurelius)

Fear follows crime and is its punishment. (Voltaire)

There is a reason it used to be a crime in the Confederate states to teach a slave to read: Literacy is power. (Matt Taibbi, American author and journalist)

Laws are like cobwebs, which may catch small flies, but let wasps and hornets break through. (Jonathan Swift)

Crime does not pay as well as politics. (Alfred E. Newman)

Nothing is illegal if a hundred businessmen decide to do it. (Andrew Young, civil rights activist and close associate of Dr. Martin Luther King, Jr.)

Make crime pay. Become a lawyer. (Will Rogers)

ENVIRONMENT

Weeds are flowers too, once you get to know them. (A. A. Milne, *Winnie-the-Pooh* author)

Dear future generations: Please accept our apologies. We were rolling drunk on petroleum. (Kurt Vonnegut)

When we go out to the country and just sit there, what we're really doing is just switching off various kinds of alertness that we don't have to use. When we do that, we are stopping being defensive. We are no longer shutting ourselves off from different types of experiences, we are welcoming them in. (Brian Eno)

And into the forest I go,
To lose my mind and find my soul. (John Muir)

We're borrowing money from China to buy oil from the Persian Gulf to burn it in ways that destroy the future of human civilization. Every bit of that has to change. (Al Gore)

For most of history, man has had to fight nature to survive; in this century he is beginning to realize that, in order to survive, he must protect it. (Jacques Cousteau)

If it's yellow; that's mellow. If it's brown; flush it down. (Camping slogan)

The earth has music for those who listen. (William Shakespeare)

Thank God, they cannot cut down the clouds. (Henry David Thoreau)

The potentially disastrous effects from higher temperature, rising sea levels, and extreme weather formations will be hugely damaging especially to the poorest and most vulnerable people on the planet. But industrialization and human activity need not produce these effects if human beings organized their activities in a planned way with due regard for the protection of natural resources and the wider impact on the environment and public health. That seems impossible under capitalism. What is really needed requires public control and ownership of the energy and transport industries and public investment in the environment for the public good. (Michael Roberts, UCLA School of Law)

Truly it may be said that the outside of a mountain is good for the inside of a man. (George Wherry, author, *Alpine Notes and the Climbing Foot*, 1896)

The best time to plant a tree was 20 years ago. The second best time is now.

To such an extent does nature delight and abound in variety that among her trees there is not one plant to be found which is exactly like another; and not only among the plants, but among the boughs, the leaves and the fruits, you will not find one which is exactly similar to another. (Leonardo da Vinci)

If there is magic on this planet it is contained in water. (Loren Eiseley)

I don't know what the future will look like, but if we are more clever than slow, we could have a radically better society in 100 years. (Gabe Cross)

Life on Earth is at the ever-increasing risk of being wiped out by a disaster, such as sudden global nuclear war, a genetically engineered virus or other dangers we have not yet thought of. (Stephen Hawking)

The biosphere feeds on itself. (Dave Cross)

The people who are out to destroy the environment think they are going to get away with it. Are they breathing different air than we're breathing? Are they eating different food? I mean, where do they think they're going to go? What do they think is going to be better than what they have destroyed? I just don't get it. (Bette Midler)

Our memories of the ocean will linger on, long after our footprints in the sand are gone. (*The Olympic Peninsula*, Craig Buhler)

You must not know too much or be too precise or scientific about birds and trees and flowers and watercraft; a certain free-margin, and even vagueness— ignorance, credulity—helps your enjoyment of these things. (Henry David Thoreau)

What season is it when you are on a trampoline?...Springtime!

Necessity is the mistress and guide of nature. Necessity is the theme and inventress of nature, her curb and her eternal law. (Leonardo da Vinci)

I'm so glad I live in a world where there are Octobers. (L. M. Montgomery, Canadian author, 1874-1942)

Herein lies our problem. If we level that much land to grow rice and whatever, then no other animal could live there except for some insect pest species. Which is very unfortunate. (Steve Irwin, Australian zookeeper, *The Crocodile Hunter*)

It was raining so hard I saw Superman riding in a cab!

The Elites—due to their wealth—do not suffer the detrimental effects of the environmental collapse until much later than the Commoners. This buffer of wealth allows Elites to continue 'business as usual' despite the impending catastrophe. (Motesharrei, Kalnay, Rivas in *Ecological Economics*)

The objective of cleaning is not just to clean, but to feel happiness living within that environment. (Marie Kondo)

Modern man's future is threatened by the world he created. (Martin Heidegger)

Rather than heralding a new era of easy living, the Agricultural Revolution left farmers with lives generally more difficult and less satisfying than those of foragers. Hunter-gatherers spent their time in more stimulating and varied ways, and were less in danger of starvation and disease; the average farmer worked harder than the average forager, and got a worse diet in return. (Yuval Noah Harrari, *Sapiens*)

Gardening is cheaper than therapy and you get tomatoes.

Our population and our use of the finite resources of planet Earth are growing exponentially, along with our technical ability to change the environment for good or ill. (Stephen Hawking)

The environment is everything that isn't me. (Albert Einstein)

I don't care what town you're born in, what city, what country. If you're a child, you are curious about your environment. You're overturning rocks. You're plucking leaves off of trees and petals off of flowers, looking inside, and you're doing things that create disorder in the lives of the adults around you. (Neil deGrasse Tyson)

People don't want to go to the dump and have a picnic, they want to go out to a beautiful place and enjoy their day. And so I think our job is to try to take the environment, take what the good Lord has given us, and expand upon it or enhance it, without destroying it. (Jack Nicklaus)

Why does the lizard stick his tongue out? The lizard sticks its tongue out because that's the way it's listening and looking and tasting its environment. Its means of appreciating what's in front of it. (William Shatner)

Chimpanzees, gorillas, orangutans have been living for hundreds of thousands of years in their forest, living fantastic lives, never overpopulating, never destroying the forest. I would say that they have been in a way more successful than us as far as being in harmony with the environment. (Jane Goodall)

The voice of the sea speaks to the soul. (Kate Chopin, 1850-1904, American author)

Forget not that the earth delights to feel your bare feet and the wind longs to play with your hair. (Kahlil Gibran)

I think the environment should be in the category of our national security. Defense of our resources is just as important as defense abroad. Otherwise, what is there to defend? (Robert Redford)

Adapt or perish, now as ever, is Nature's inexorable imperative. (H. G. Wells)

RING BELL. Pull weeds until someone answers. (Doormat)

If I were a tree, I'd have no reason to love a human.
 (Maggie Steifvater, *The Raven Boys*)

There's over a billion people on this planet that don't
have access to clean drinking water. (Michael Moore)

Have you ever noticed that they put advertisements in
with your bills now? Like bills aren't distasteful enough,
they have to stuff junk mail in there with them. I get back
at them. I put garbage in with my check when I mail it in.
Coffee grounds, banana peels. I write: "Could you throw
these away for me? Thank you." (Andy Rooney)

Rivers run in only one direction. Oceans run in two.

Have you ever noticed how quiet you get when you go
into the woods? It's almost like you know that God's
there. (Richard Pryor)

It's been proven by quite a few studies that plants are
good for our psychological development. If you green an
area, the rate of crime goes down. Torture victims begin
to recover when they spend time outside in a garden
with flowers. So we need them, in some deep
psychological sense, which I don't suppose anybody
really understands yet. (Jane Goodall)

Terror acts in the same manner on animals as on us,
causing the muscles to tremble, the heart to palpitate,
the sphincters to be relaxed, and the hair to stand on
end. (Charles Darwin)

I love to think of nature as an unlimited broadcasting
system through which God speaks to us every hour, if
we will only tune him in. (George Washington Carver)

The sky is filled with stars, invisible by day. (Henry
Wordsworth Longfellow)

Autumn is a second spring when every leaf is a flower.
  (Albert Camus)

Not one would mind, neither bird nor tree,
If mankind perished utterly,
And Spring, herself, when she woke at dawn,
Would scarcely know that we were gone.
  (Sara Teasdale, 1884-1933, American poet)

EVERYDAY

In the amusement park of life we don't take the rides, the rides take us. (Richard Farrell, *Born of Silence,* 1990)

We should never judge a day by its weather. (Dick Van Dyke)

Things turn out best for the people who make the best of the way things turn out. (John Wooden)

Don't try so hard to fit in, and certainly don't try so hard to be different. Just try hard to be you. (Zendaya, American actress, *The Greatest Show on Earth*)

Everyone is brave when there is nothing at stake.

I tell you, we are here on Earth to fart around, and don't let anybody tell you different. (Kurt Vonnegut)

Don't let the same dog bite you twice. (Chuck Berry)

Never a failure, always a lesson. (Rihanna)

Do not be angry with the rain; it simply does not know how to fall upwards. (Vladimir Nabokov)

Build your own dreams; or someone else will hire you to build theirs. (Farrah Gray)

My momma always said, "Life is like a box of chocolates. You never know what you're gonna get." (Winston Groom, *Forrest Gump*, 1994)

I'm confident that I am as intelligent as many people, but I know that I'm not as intelligent as some. So in the presence of hyper intelligent people, I'm a shrinking violet because I don't want to look like a fool. I know a little about a lot and a lot about a little. (Bette Midler)

Never underestimate the length of a shortcut. (Claudia Jernigan)

It can be a real struggle to accept that sometimes appearance can be more important than talent or intelligence. (Jennifer Hudson, American singer and actress)

Be polite to all, but intimate with few. (Thomas Jefferson)

First things first, I'm da realest. (Iggy Azalea)

I've learned that people will forget what you said, people will forget what you did, but people will never forget how you made them feel. (Maya Angelou)

We are supposed to enjoy the good stuff now, while we can, with the people we love. Life has a funny way of teaching us that lesson over and over again. (Sheena Easton)

Cleanliness becomes more important when godliness becomes unlikely. (P. J. O'Rourke)

I make mistakes, I'll be the second to admit it. (Jean Kerr, 1922-2003, Irish-American author and playwright)

What a strange illusion it is to suppose that beauty is goodness. (Leo Tolstoy)

People seem not to see that their opinion of the world is also a confessor of character. (Ralph Waldo Emerson)

I don't trust anyone who doesn't laugh. (Maya Angelou)

The reason I talk to myself is that I'm the only one whose answers I accept. (George Carlin)

I am aware, as everybody has to be, that there's more competition for one's attention nowadays. (Tom Stoppard)

Thieves and scholars look the same. (Japanese proverb)

Stay gold. (Johnny's dying words in *The Outsiders,* S. E. Hinton, 1967)

You have to do your own growing no matter how tall your grandfather was. (Abraham Lincoln)

Imperfection is underrated. Perfection is overrated. (Helena Bonham Carter, English actress)

It ain't what you don't know that gets you in trouble. It's the things you know for sure that ain't so. (Mark Twain)

It is easier to catch a runaway horse than take back a spoken word. (Mongolian proverb)

All the mistakes I ever made were when I wanted to say 'No" and said 'Yes.' (Moss Hart, 1904-61, American playwright and theatre director)

The church is near, but the way is icy. The tavern is far, but I will walk carefully. (Ukrainian proverb)

A free life cannot acquire many possessions, because this is not easy to do without servility to mobs or monarchs. (Epicurus)

It's hard to get lost when you don't know where you're going. (Jim Jarmusch, filmmaker)

Fools and scissors require careful handling. (Japanese proverb)

Every day is a new opportunity. You can build on yesterday's success or put its failures behind and start over again. That's the way life is, with a new game every day, and that's the way baseball is. (Bob Feller)

Some days you're the kid with the stick, some days you're the piñata. (Alec Baldwin)

If you look like a donkey they'll put a load on your back. (Mongolian proverb)

As the vilest writer hath his readers, so the greatest liar hath his believers: and it often happens, that if a lie be believed only for an hour, it hath done its work. (Jonathan Swift)

Never squat with your spurs on. (Texan proverb)

Abstaining is favorable both to the head and the pocket. (W. C. Fields)

The madness of individuals is an exception. The madness of groups, parties, nations and epochs is a rule. (Frederic Nietzsche)

The past is an old armchair in the attic, the present an ominous ticking sound, and the future is anybody's guess. (James Thurber)

Abuse often starts with praise. (Japanese proverb)

Nothing in all the world is more dangerous than sincere ignorance and conscientious stupidity. (Martin Luther King Jr.)

Man's mind is so formed that it is far more susceptible to falsehood than to truth. (Desiderius Erasmus,1466-1536, Dutch scholar)

I don't want to be a pessimist. I'm a realist. One man's realist is another man's pessimist. (Bill Maher)

Life is short. Kiss slowly, laugh insanely, love truly, and forgive quickly. (Paulo Coelho, Brazilian lyricist and novelist)

My head's never really quiet. The only time I can get it to turn off is if I watch *CSI* or *Law and Order*, where I have to follow the crime. If I can't turn my head off during that, I know I've really got a problem. (Taylor Swift)

That it will never come again is what makes life sweet. (Emily Dickenson)

You gotta try your luck at least once a day, because you could be going around lucky all day and not even know it. (Jimmy Dean)

Even the street dog has his lucky days. (Japanese proverb)

If you destroy a bridge, be sure you can swim. (Swahili Culture)

Be where you are; otherwise you will miss your life. (Buddha)

There's nothing noble in being superior to your fellow man. True nobility lies in being superior to your former self. (Ernest Hemingway)

Don't talk unless you can improve the silence. (Jorge Luis Borges)

It's a terrible waste to be happy and not notice it. (Kurt Vonnegut)

Normality is a paved road. It's comfortable to walk, but no flowers grow on it. (Vincent van Gogh)

The mind is not a vessel to be filled, but a fire to be kindled. (Plutarch, 45-127 A.D., Greek biographer)

The world will ask who you are, and if you don't know, the world will tell you. (Carl Yung)

Truth is proper and beautiful at all times and in all places. (Frederick Douglass)

All human beings have three lives: public, private, and secret. (Gabriel Garcia Marquez)

Knowledge speaks, but wisdom listens. (Jimi Hendrix)

Don't let one cloud obliterate the whole sky. (Anais Nin)

Happiness makes up in height for what it lacks in length. (Robert Frost)

You will never reach your destination if you stop and throw stones at every dog that barks. (Winston Churchill)

If you're the smartest person in the entire room, you're in the wrong room. (Taylor Swift)

My purpose in life does not include a hankering to charm society. (James Dean)

The ingenuity of self-deception is inexhaustible. (Hannah More, 1745-1833, English religious writer and philanthropist)

God gave us mouths that close and ears that don't…that should tell us something. (Eugene O'Neil)

A well-spent day brings happy sleep. (Leonardo da Vinci)

It's a sign of great inner insecurity to be hostile to the unfamiliar. (Anais Nin)

Success comes before work only in the dictionary.

Be as you wish to seem. (Socrates)

Self-discipline is doing one small thing at a time. (Sonjah)

Listening, not imitation, may be the sincerest form of flattery. (Joyce Brothers)

The important thing is to be in love with something. (Ray Bradbury)

I hear and I forget. I see and I remember. I do and I understand. (Confucius)

Television is bubble-gum for the mind. (Frank Lloyd Wright, 1867-1959, American architect)

Acclaim is a distraction. (James Broughton, 1913-1999, American poet and filmmaker)

A sinner can reform, but stupid is forever. (Alan Jay Lerner, 1918-1986, American lyricist and librettist)

Inspiration exists, but it has to find us working. (Pablo Picasso)

Most people work just hard enough not to get fired and get paid just enough money not to quit. (George Carlin)

Just because you're paranoid doesn't mean they're not out to get you. (Richard Nixon)

I second-guess and overthink and rethink every single thing I do. (Taylor Swift)

Fear an ignorant man more than a lion. (Turkish proverb)

One of the advantages of being disorderly is that one is constantly making exciting discoveries. (A. A. Milne)

Every time you clean something, you just make something else dirty.

I think I'm constantly in a state of adjustment. (Patti Smith)

Bad things happen when good people pretend nothing is wrong. (Corey Taylor)

Employ your time in improving yourself by other men's writings, so that you shall gain easily what others have labored hard for. (Socrates)

There is nothing in which people more betray their character than in what they laugh at. (Johann Wolfgang von Goethe)

Stop trying to make everybody happy. You're not tequila. (Gas station sandwich board)

If 40 million people say a foolish thing it does not become a wise one. (W. Somerset Maugham)

If you read somebody's diary, you get what you deserve.
(David Sedaris)

It is absurd to divide people into good and bad. People
are either charming or tedious. (Oscar Wilde)

Give me six hours to chop down a tree and I will spend
the first four sharpening the axe. (Abraham Lincoln)

If you do what you've always done, you'll get what
you've always gotten. (Tony Robbins)

You're never wrong to do the right thing. (Mark Twain)

Never give a sword to a man who can't dance.
(Confucius)

Silence is all the genius a fool has. (Zora Neale Hurston)

It is more fun to talk with someone who doesn't use long,
difficult words but rather short, easy words, like 'what
about lunch?' (A. A. Milne)

FASHION

Fashions come and go; bad taste is timeless. (Beau Brummell)

Some of the worst mistakes of my life have been haircuts. (Jim Morrison, lead singer in The Doors)

I have flabby thighs, but fortunately my stomach covers them. (Joan Rivers)

Fashion is what goes out of fashion. (Coco Chanel)

Fashion is gentility running away from vulgarity and afraid of being overtaken. (William Hazlitt)

Fashion is, for the most part, nothing but the ostentation of riches. (John Locke)

Never leave a rhinestone unturned. (Dolly Parton)

I feel like the worst fashion moments of the 90's were kind of the best. (Charli XCX)

A narcissist is someone better looking than you are. (Gore Vidal)

Good breeding consists of concealing how much we think of ourselves and how little we think of the other person. (Mark Twain)

You're only as good as your last haircut. (Fran Lebowitz, American author, public speaker)

Whoever said money can't buy happiness didn't know where to shop. (Gertrude Stein)

It's not what you're wearing, it's the way you wear it. (Pharrell Williams)

My friend, Sue Ann, in college pulled me aside and said, "Honey I love you but you have got to start waxing your eyebrows. They look wild!" So thank you, that kinda changed my life. (Angela Kinsey, American actress)

I just feel my best when I'm all glammed up. (Kim Kardashian)

I think Led Zeppelin must have worn some of the most peculiar clothing that men had ever been seen to wear without cracking a smile. (Robert Plant, lead singer in Led Zeppelin)

Please don't wear skinny jeans if you don't have skinny genes. (Seth Rogan)

I'm a big woman. I need big hair. (Aretha Franklin)

Wearing of the Fez hat is illegal in Turkey, having been banned in 1925.

I remember when I was in high school I didn't have a new dress for each special occasion. The girls would bring the fact to my attention, not always too delicately. The boys, however, never bothered with the subject. They were my friends, not because of the size of my wardrobe but because they liked me. (Marilyn Monroe)

I firmly believe that with the right footwear one can rule the world. (Bette Midler)

Cock your hat. Angles are attitudes. (Frank Sinatra)

I've never had my hair cut by anybody. I do it all myself. (Keith Richards)

71

I go to these photo-shoots, and each time I figure out something new about myself and what I want to wear.
(Taylor Swift)

I love the way little kids dress themselves. They're completely carefree about how others perceive them.
(Gillian Zinser, American actress)

You'd be surprised how much it costs to look this cheap!
(Dolly Parton)

FOOD

One thing I like about Argentina, they only cook with salt; that's it. (Robert Duvall)

My doctor told me to stop having intimate dinners for four. Unless there are three other people. (Orson Welles)

Café mi Vida (Coffee, my Life). (Ry Miller)

I'm blessed with a terrible pallet: cheap wine tastes fine to me. (Dave Cross)

How come when you mix flour and water together you get glue, and then you add eggs and sugar and you get cake? Where does the glue go? (Rita Rudner)

Good broth will resurrect the dead. (South American proverb)

Sixty percent of the vegetables you see in the supermarkets came from the American Indians. They also gave us aspirin and quinine. And their model of government parallels our Senate. But their women elected the chiefs, and impeached them. (Harry Dean Stanton, 1926-2017, American actor, musician, and singer)

Tea! Bless ordinary everyday afternoon tea. (Agatha Christie)

In Mexico, girls just want to have flan. (Douglas Miller)

Wine is bottled poetry. (Robert Louis Stevenson)

Best way to get rid of kitchen odors: eat out. (Phyllis Diller)

73

Coffee in England always tastes like a chemistry experiment. (Agatha Christie)

The 5 levels of fatness: Big, healthy, husky, fluffy and damn. (Gabriel Iglesias)

You live by the cake, you die by the cake. (Gabriel Iglesias)

When I'm no longer rapping, I want to open up an ice cream parlor and call myself Scoop Dogg. (Snoop Dogg)

New Rule: Food companies must face the facts. One container equals one serving. Look, we're Americans, and that means once we open the bag, there's no stopping us until we're licking stray bits of powdered cheese off the carpet. So stop trying to give us nutritional information based on a fraction of the package. It assumes a talent for two things that we're really not capable of: restraint and math. (Bill Maher)

The laziest man I ever met put popcorn in his pancakes so they would turn over by themselves. (W. C. Fields)

I think many cooks are afraid of undercooked meats. A good thermometer is a cook's best friend. (Emeril Lagasse)

I used to help my granddaddy make sausage. He would mix it up in a cleaned-out washtub with his hands, no gloves. Man, if we did anything like that today, they would jack the jail up and throw us under it. (Jimmy Dean, 1928-2010, American country singer, TV personality and creator of "Jimmy Dean Sausage" products)

I love things that are indescribable, like the taste of an avocado or the smell of a gardenia. (Barbra Streisand)

My favorite food from my homeland is Guinness. My second choice is Guinness. My third choice…would have to be Guinness. (Peter O'Toole)

Hamburgers taste better in outer space because they're meteor. (T-shirt)

I work out to eat. (Bobby Flay)

About 74% of all habitat destruction on the planet is either caused directly for livestock or to grow feed for livestock. (Chris Darwin, great, great grandson of Charles Darwin)

One drink is just right; two is too many; three are too few. (Spanish proverb)

Spaghetti can be eaten most successfully if you inhale it like a vacuum cleaner. (Sophia Loren)

My theory is that all of Scottish cuisine is based on a dare. (Mike Myers, Canadian actor, comedian, screenwriter, and film producer)

How about that McDonald's two blocks from Ground Zero? That's killed more people than the 19 hijackers. (Michael Moore)

What's a soup kitchen? (Paris Hilton)

I was going to McDonald's and Taco Bell every day. The kids behind the counter knew me—it wouldn't even phase them. Or I'd sit up at Denny's or Big Boy and just eat by myself. It was sad. I got so heavy that people started to not recognize me. (Eminem)

I was a vegetarian until I started leaning toward the sunlight. (Rita Rudner)

Peanuts are one of the ingredients in dynamite.

What do you get when you cross a credit card and a steamed-brewed coffee?...American Espresso.

Wise-men talk about ideas; intellectuals of facts; and the common man of food. (Mongolian proverb)

A hot dog at the game beats roast beef at the Ritz. (Humphrey Bogart)

The introduction to cooking may well have been the decisive factor in leading man from a primarily animal existence into one that was more fully human. (Carlton S. Coon, American physical and cultural anthropologist)

I think about food literally all day every day. It's a thing. (Taylor Swift)

TV cameras seem to add ten pounds to me. So I make it a policy never to eat TV cameras. (Kitty Carlisle, 1910-2007, actress, panelist on *To Tell The Truth*)

Whenever I drink champagne I either laugh or cry...I love champagne. (Tina Turner)

There's not a man, woman or child on the face of the earth who doesn't enjoy a tasty beverage. (David Letterman)

Never doubt the courage of the French. They were the ones who discovered that snails are edible. (Doug Larson, American columnist and editor)

76

I've just opened a new restaurant called "Karma."
There's no menu, we just give you what you deserve.

MYTHAI (License Plate)

For the first time ever, overweight people outnumber
average people in America. You're average...hey, let's
get a pizza. (Jay Leno)

I got the blues thinking of the future, so I left off and
made some marmalade. It's amazing how it cheers one
up to shred oranges and scrub the floor. (D.H.
Lawrence)

Cooking with kids is not just about ingredients, recipes,
and cooking, It's about harnessing imagination,
empowerment, and creativity. (Guy Fieri, American
restaurateur, author, television host)

My absolute favorite meal in Nashville is sweet-potato
pancakes at Pancake Pantry. (Taylor Swift)

Recipe? Recipe? We don' need no stinkin' recipe. (Eli
Wallach)

GENDER

The feminine in the man is the sugar in the whiskey. The masculine in the woman is the yeast in the bread. Without these ingredients the result is flat, without tang or flavor. (Edna Ferber)

I'm not offended by all the dumb-blonde jokes because I know I'm not dumb...and I also know that I'm not blonde. (Dolly Parton)

I'm a gay man trapped in a woman's body. (Madonna Ciccone)

The reason the All-American boy prefers beauty to brains is that he can see better than he can think. (Farrah Fawcett)

I choose a man who compels my strength, who makes enormous demands on me, who does not doubt my courage or my toughness, who does not believe me naive or innocent, who has the courage to treat me like a woman. (Anais Nin)

We hold these truths to be self-evident: that all men and women are created equal. (Elizabeth Cady Stanton, 1815-1902, Women's rights activist)

Women will never be as successful as men because they have no wives to advise them. (Dick Van Dyke)

Aviation, this young modern giant, exemplifies the possible relationship of women and the creations of science. Although women have not taken full advantage of its use and benefits, air travel is as available to them as to men. (Amelia Earhart)

78

Women are made to be loved, not understood. (Oscar Wilde)

Plain women know more about men than beautiful women do. (Katherine Hepburn)

There are three kinds of men. The one who learns by reading. The few who learn by observation. The rest of them have to pee on the electric fence for themselves. (Will Rogers)

Women should be obscene and not heard. (Groucho Marx)

Claiming that someone's marriage is against your religion is like being angry at someone for eating a donut because you're on a diet. (Seth Rogan)

Once made equal to man, woman becomes his superior. (Socrates, 470-399 B.C.)

I never felt oppressed because of my gender. When I'm writing a poem or drawing, I'm not a female; I'm an artist. (Patti Smith)

A woman is like a teabag; you can't tell how strong she is until you put her in hot water. (Eleanor Roosevelt)

There are only two types of women: goddesses and doormats. (Pablo Picasso)

Writing books is the closest men ever come to childbearing. (Norman Mailer)

A man is commanding; a woman demanding. A man is forceful; a woman is pushy. A man is uncompromising; a woman is a ball-breaker. A man is a perfectionist; a woman is a pain in the ass. He's assertive; she's aggressive. He strategizes; she manipulates. He shows leadership; she's controlling. He's committed; she's obsessed. He's persevering; she's relentless. He sticks to his guns; she's stubborn. If a man wants to get it right, he's looked up to and respected. If a woman wants to get it right, she's difficult and impossible. (Barbra Streisand)

A woman would never make a nuclear bomb. They would never make a weapon that kills–no, no. They'd make a weapon that makes you feel bad for a while. (Robin Williams)

Balls are to men what purses are to women. (Sarah Jessica Parker)

I've learned a lot about women. I think I've learned exactly how the fall of man occurred in the Garden of Eden. Adam and Eve were in the Garden of Eden, and Adam said one day, 'Wow, Eve, here we are, at one with nature, at one with God, we'll never age, we'll never die, and all our dreams come true the instant that we have them.' And Eve said, 'Yeah…it's just not enough is it?' (Bill Hicks, 1961-1994, American stand-up comedian, social critic, satirist and musician)

It is really a hard life. Men will not be nice to you if you are not good looking, and women will not be nice to you if you are. (Agatha Christie)

I think it is about time that equipped women begin to take on some of the ethical questions which a male-dominated culture has produced and dissect and analyze them quite to pieces in a serious fashion. It is time that 'half the human race' had something to say about the nature of its existence. (Lorraine Hansberry, African-American playwright)

Of course I know Julie Andrews. She's the last of the really great broads. (Paul Newman)

You're not too smart, are you? I like that in a man. (Kathleen Turner)

Men Are from Mars, Women Are from Venus. (Book title, John Gray, 1992)

Strong is the New Pretty. (Book title, Kate T. Parker, 2017)

HOLIDAYS

Father's Day: when you get that lethal combination of alcohol and power tools. (David Letterman)

What do you eat on July 5th?...Independence Day-old pizza. (*AARP Magazine*)

I celebrate everyone's religious holidays. If it's good enough for the righteous, it's good enough for the self-righteous, I always say. (Bette Midler)

Fake Christmas trees have been found for 20 years to be more environmentally friendly than real trees.

Ah, my dad's whistle. On holidays when I was a kid, we would all be off in the rock pools along the beach. When it came time to go, we'd hear the whistle and we'd all come running. Like dogs! (Kate Winslet)

My father was so cheap: For Easter, we'd wear the same clothes, but he'd take us to a different church.
  (A.J. Jamal, American actor, comedian)

Yesterday was the Winter Solstice. I celebrated it by going to bed early. (Mike Bethard)

I don't think Christmas is necessarily about things. It's about being good to one another, it's about the Christian epic, it's about kindness. (Carrie Fisher)

As you know, Labor Day is the day we honor hard-working people in America. So let's take a moment to thank all those people by saying, "Gracias, Amigos!"
  (Jay Leno)

On Halloween I ran out of candy and had to give out nicotine gum. (David Letterman)

There is nothing sadder in this world than to awake Christmas morning and not be a child. (Erma Bombeck)

JIVE & CHOPS

I never forget a face, but in your case I'll make an exception. (Groucho Marx)

Large and in charge.

That's for true! (Justin Wilson, Louisiana chef & humorist, *Gumbo* on YouTube)

I gar-on-TEE! (Justin Wilson)

I'll see you tomorrow…
Thanks for the warning (or)
Not if I see you first

If your brains were dynamite there wouldn't be enough to blow your hat off. (Kurt Vonnegut)

What's the biggy, Miss Piggy?

Go tell your mother she wants to see you.

Let's make like a tree and leave.

Don't quit your day job.

If silence were golden,
You couldn't raise a dime,
Because your mind is on vacation
And your mouth is working overtime.
  (Mose Allison, *Your Mind is on Vacation*, 1976)

KID JOKES

What do get when you cross a cheetah with a hamburger?...Fast Food. (Simon & Teyo Miller)

Where do hamburgers go to dance?...They go to the meatball.

Why can't your nose be 12 inches long?...Because then it would be a foot.

Where do sheep go to get haircuts?...The baa-baa shop.

What kind of bird never needs a haircut?...A Bald Eagle.

What's the most musical part of a chicken?...The drumstick.

Knock, knock
Who's there?
Canoe
Canoe who?
Canoe help me with my homework?

Knock, knock
Who's there?
Spell
Spell who
W-H-O

What do you call a bear with no teeth?...A gummy bear.

What creature is smarter than a talking parrot?...A spelling bee.

What did the fisherman say to the magician?...Pick a cod, any cod.

What do elves learn at school?...The elfabet.

Where do cows go for entertainment?...The moooo-vies.

What did the bottle of ranch say when somebody opened the refrigerator?..."Shut that door! I'm dressing!"

How do you know that carrots are good for your eyesight?...Have you ever seen a rabbit wearing glasses?

What's a cheerleader's favorite drink?...Root beer.

Where does a polar bear keep his money?...In a snow bank.

What do you call a king that is only 12 inches tall?...A ruler.

How do you measure grass?...With a yardstick. (*AARP Magazine*)

When I was young there were only 25 letters in the alphabet. Nobody knew why.

What music are balloons scared of?...Pop music.

What does a shark like to eat with peanut butter?...Jellyfish.

What kind of crackers do firemen like in their soup?...Firecrackers!

Why did the birdie go to the hospital?...To get a tweetment.

What did the mama cow say to the baby cow?...It's pasture bedtime. (Brooke Gen)

What do cats eat for breakfast?...Mice Krispies.

What does a triceratops sit on?...It's Tricera-bottom.

Knock, knock
Who's there?
Ya
Ya who?
I just knew we were going to have a good time!

What do carpenters hate to hit?...Finger-nails.

What do you call a cow that plays guitar?...a Moo-sician. (Nicole)

What did one eye say to the other?...Between you and me, something smells around here. (*AARP magazine*)

I've never worked out what the moral of Humpty Dumpty is. I can only think of: Don't sit on a wall if you're an egg. (Rick Gervais)

Will you remember me in one minute?
Sure
Knock, knock.
Who's there?
You've forgotten me already!

LOVE

Love is the wild card of existence. (Rita Mae Brown, American writer, activist, and feminist)

My lover asks me, "What is the difference between me and the sky?" The difference, my love, is that when you laugh, I forget about the sky. (Nizar Qabbani, 1923–1998,Syrian diplomat, poet and publisher)

The moon is a friend for the lonesome to talk to. (Carl Sandburg)

The only way to get love is to be lovable. It's very irritating if you have a lot of money. You'd like to think you could write a check: 'I'll buy a million dollars' worth of love.' But it doesn't work that way. The more you give love away the more you get. (Warren Buffett)

In the pursuit of pleasure there is no difference between a woman and a man. (Japanese proverb)

Only a man who has loved a woman of genius can appreciate what happiness there is in loving a fool. (Talleyrand, 1754--1838, French bishop, politician, and diplomat)

For a few seconds they looked silently into each other's eyes, and the distant and impossible suddenly became near, possible, and inevitable. (Leo Tolstoy)

People who care about each other enjoy doing things for one another. They don't consider it servitude. (Ann Landers)

In the arithmetic of love, one plus one equals everything, and two minus one equals nothing. (Mignon McLaughlin, 1913-1983, American journalist and author)

Love is like a brick. You can build a house, or you can sink a dead body. (Lady Gaga)

You know, when it works, love is pretty amazing. It's not overrated. There's a reason for all those songs. (Sarah Dessen, American novelist)

I've only been in love with a beer bottle and a mirror. (Sid Vicious)

Love is like the wind; you can't see it but you can feel it. (Nicholas Sparks, American novelist and screenwriter)

Love unlocks doors and opens windows that weren't even there before. (Mignon McLaughlin)

Love is, above all, a gift of oneself. (Jean Anouilh, French dramatist, *Antigone,* 1944)

I knew I had fallen in love with Lolita forever, but I also knew she would not be forever Lolita. (Vladimir Nabokov)

I think true romance is dry schizophrenic...but life would be so boring without true love. (Charli XCX)

Not one word, not one gesture of yours shall I, could I, ever forget. (Leo Tolstoy)

Someone said, 'I love you' and it scared me half to death. (Will Brady, *The Real New Ground,* 1997)

Love is of all passions the strongest, for it attacks simultaneously the head, the heart and the senses. (Lao Tzu)

Civilized people cannot fully satisfy their sexual instinct without love. (Bertrand Russell)

If love is blind, why is lingerie so popular? (Dorothy Parker)

It's so easy to love. The only hard thing is to be loved. (Vincent van Gogh)

Love is friendship set on fire. (Greeting card)

I learned the truth at seventeen,
That love was meant for beauty queens,
And high school girls with clear skinned smiles,
Who married young and then retired. (Janis Ian, *At Seventeen*, 1975)

Never strike your wife, even with a flower. (Indian proverb)

People who throw kisses are hopelessly lazy. (Bob Hope)

Love is the beauty of the soul. (Saint Augustine)

For 'twas not into my ear you whispered but into my heart. 'Twas not my lips you kissed, but my soul.' (Judy Garland)

Love is overrated. Biochemically no different than eating large quantities of chocolate. (Al Pacino)

Country love song: "It's hard to kiss the lips at night that chewed my ass all day." (Mike Bethard)

Love is a friendship set to music. (John Campbell)

The giving of love is an education in itself. (Eleanor Roosevelt)

Love is a great beautifier. (Louisa May Alcott)

Falling out of love is like losing weight. It's a lot easier putting it on than taking it off. (Aretha Franklin)

Among those whom I like and admire, I can find no common denominator, but among those whom I love, I can: all of them make me laugh. (W. H. Auden)

What I have always loved most in men is imperfection. I get moved by the wrinkles on the throat of a man. It makes me love him more. I think it is sad that more women don't take the chance that maybe men will be moved by seeing the chin a little less firm than it used to be, that a man will be more in love with his wife because he remembers who she was and sees who she is and thinks, God, isn't it lovely that this happened to her, and be moved by life telling its story there. (Liv Ullman)

Knock, knock
Who's there
Olive
Olive who?
Olive you.

MEDICINE

Researcher 1: Is it true you've found the gene that causes doubt?
Researcher 2: I'm not sure.

I like nonsense; it wakes up the brain cells. (Dr. Seuss)

I suppose that when ants get stepped on, they have no idea what hit them. But I'll bet that hasn't stopped them from coming up with fancy names for it, like "spontaneous compression" or "vertical planar syndrome." (Lemel Herbert-Williams)

I got the bill for my surgery. Now I know why those doctors were wearing masks. (James H. Boren, 1925–2010, American humorist)

Nature, time and patience are the three great physicians. (Chinese proverb)

Though the doctors treated him, let his blood, and gave him medications to drink, he nevertheless recovered.

Asthma doesn't seem to bother me any more unless I'm around cigars or dogs. The thing that would bother me most would be a dog smoking a cigar. (Steve Allen)

Always laugh when you can. It is cheap medicine. (Lord Byron)

I'm not an alcoholic, I only drink two times a year. When it's my birthday, and when it's not my birthday. (Bill Murray)

Health overweighs all other blessings so much that one can really say that a healthy beggar is happier than an ailing king. (Arthur Schopenhauer)

I'm in shape. Round is a shape. (George Carlin)

No man is a good physician who has never been sick.
(Arabian proverb)

I mean some doctor told me I had six months to live and
I went to their funeral. (Keith Richards)

America's healthcare system is second only to Japan,
Canada, Sweden, Great Britain...well, all of Europe. But
you can thank your lucky stars we don't live in Paraguay!
(Homer Simpson)

He who eats when full, digs his own grave with his teeth.
(Turkish proverb)

Some people think that doctors and nurses can put
scrambled eggs back into the shell. (Dorothy Canfield
Fisher, 1879-1958, educational reformer, social activist,
American author)

Subdue your appetites, my dears, and you've conquered
human nature. (Dorothy Canfield Fisher)

I'm scared to death of being stone cold sober. (Jerry Lee
Lewis)

Variety is what I would recommend. As variety is the
spice of life in food, so it is in exercise. Change it up. But
most of all, don't overdo it. (Martina Navratilova,
legendary tennis player)

The great secret of doctors...still hidden from the
public...is that most things get better by themselves.
(Lewis Thomas, 1913-1993, American physician, poet)

More people die from eating too much than from
starving. (Hebrew proverb)

I have kleptomania, but when it gets bad, I take something for it. (Robert Benchley)

To live long, live slowly. (Markus Tullius Cicero, 106-43 B.C., Roman statesman)

My doctor told me that jogging could add years to my life. I think he was right. I feel ten years older already. (Milton Berle)

An apple a day keeps the doctor away. (Benjamin Franklin)

Whatever you do, always give 100%. Unless you're donating blood. (Bill Murray)

Measles make you bumpy
And mumps will make you lumpy
And chicken pox'll make you jump and twitch
A common cold'll fool ya
And whooping cough'll cool ya
But poison ivy, Lord'll make you itch.
  (Jerry Lieber & Mike Stoller, *Poison Ivy*, 1958)

METAPHORS

Like rearranging the deck chairs on the Titanic
You can't get the toothpaste back in the tube
It's a food fight
It was a train wreck
She's been around the block
A can of worms
Throw someone under the bus
A double-edged sword
Cut off your nose to spite your face
Go off the rails
You can't un-ring a bell
It's like putting lipstick on a pig
That train has left the station.
It'll be like shooting fish in a barrel
The elephant in the room
He lives in a bubble
That's just the tip of the iceberg
He was hung out to dry
A "Hail Mary" pass
The brass ring
Something's coming down the pike
Pull back the curtain
The walls are closing in
He's knee deep in trouble
There's no strings attached
Put your money where your mouth is
He's a Monday morning quarterback
Fold up your tent
Ride off into the sunset
He's in bed with so-and-so
A nail in the coffin
It's a political hot potato
Pregnant pause
It's a jump ball
A shot in the dark
A warning shot fired over the bow

Put the cart before the horse
The calm before the storm
A pain in the neck
Bearing fruit
We see the fallout
They smell blood
The defendant flipped
Falling on your sword
Dead in the water
Paint yourself into a corner
I can see the writing on the wall
Let's see if it sticks to the wall
A nothing burger
They're playing hardball
It's in the bag
Shoot yourself in the foot
I'm in hot water
You can talk until you're blue in the face
Don't throw out the baby with the bathwater
It left a bad taste in my mouth
Spill the beans
Let the cat out of the bag
Red herring
Drill down
Make the trains run on time
Cut off at the knees
It's off to the races
I'm up against the wall
Trophy wife
She has a bee in her bonnet
Work your fingers to the bone
It's like pouring gasoline on a fire
It's coming full circle
Full tilt
Take something off the table
It's coming home to roost
Hold their feet to the fire
Slippery slope

It doesn't pass the smell test
A fly on the wall
Rose colored glasses
It's like trying to fit a square peg into a round hole
It might come back to bite you on the ass/butt
Jump on the bandwagon
Punt
I don't want to steal your thunder
He's got something up his sleeve
Put a lid on it
Money laundering
Bend over backwards
Who will blink first
Barking up the wrong tree
Rob Peter to pay Paul
It's Greek to me
But he didn't pull the trigger
He has an itchy trigger finger
Now the shoe is on the other foot
Waiting for the other shoe to drop
The only game in town
A rotten apple in the barrel
The buck stops here
Two ships passing in the night
Let me know when the dust clears
It's just a drop in the bucket
It will never see the light of day
Smoking gun
The bottom of the barrel
Toss your cookies
Go through the roof
A level playing field
Keep your fingers crossed
The carrot and/or the stick
Get taken to the cleaners
Light at the end of the tunnel
Who's going to blink first
Get your foot in the door

A red herring
He can't walk and chew gum
The poster child for...
Everything but the kitchen sink
You don't have to reinvent the wheel
Don't let him take you for a ride
I'm so hungry I could eat a horse
Have your cake and eat it too
The proof is in the pudding
Show you the ropes
You put your finger on it
He missed the boat
I've got your back
He's got an axe to grind
Bigger fish to fry
You're my ace in the hole
Keep your eyes peeled
Elvis has left the building
It's all water under the bridge
He's a shoe-in
In hot water
It's got your name written all over it
It blows them all away
The I's still need to be dotted, and the T's still need to be crossed
That's a different ball game
Batten down the hatches
Circle the wagons
Fasten your seatbelts
They'll have his head on a platter
It's a long road to hoe
Now the cat is out of the bag
Head them off at the pass
If it walks like a duck...
A deer in the headlights
Everything handed to him on a platter
Bring home the bacon
It's my bread and butter

Button your lip
Watch him like a hawk
A hill of beans

MONEY

Buddy, can you spare a dime?...Sure...you got change for a twenty? (Tom Newbill)

They usually have two tellers at my local bank, except when it's very busy, when they have one. (Rita Rudner)

I was born with a plastic spoon in my mouth, (Pete Townshend of The Who)

In this country you're guilty until proven wealthy. (Bill Maher)

Greed can overtake smart. (Bill Maher)

You want 21 percent risk free? Pay off your credit cards. (Andrew Tobias)

The United Way realized that it had never received a donation from the city's most successful lawyer. So a United Way worker paid the lawyer a visit in his lavish office. The United Way guy opened the meeting by saying, 'Our research shows that even though your annual income is over two million dollars, you don't give a penny to charity. Wouldn't you like to give something back to your community through the United Way?' The lawyer thinks for a minute and says, 'First, did your research also show you that my mother is dying after a long, painful illness and she has huge medical bills that are far beyond her ability to pay?' Embarrassed, the United Way rep mumbles, 'Uh... no, I didn't know that.' 'Secondly,' says the lawyer, 'did it show that my brother, a disabled veteran, is blind and confined to a wheelchair and is unable to support his wife and six children? The stricken United Way rep begins to stammer an apology, but is cut off again. 'Thirdly, did your research also show you that my sister's husband died in a dreadful car accident, leaving her penniless with a mortgage and three children, one of whom is disabled and another that has learning disabilities requiring an array of private tutors?' The humiliated United Way rep, completely beaten, says, 'I'm so sorry. I had no idea.' And the lawyer says, 'So, if I didn't give any money to them, what makes you think I'd give any to you?'

If you make a habit of buying things you do not need, you will soon be selling things you do. (Philippine proverb)

The fool who owns an ox is seldom recognized as a fool. (South African proverb)

I never had a penny to my name. So I changed my name. (Henny Youngman)

The idea of *'Spoonful'* was that it doesn't take a large quantity of anything to be good. If you have a little money when you need it, you're right there in the right spot, that'll buy you a whole lot. (Howlin' Wolf)

To understand that money doesn't buy happiness doesn't necessarily make anyone happier with less money.

All you need in this life is ignorance and confidence, and then success is sure. (Mark Twain)

What's money? A man is a success if he gets up in the morning and goes to bed at night and in between does what he wants to do. (Bob Dylan)

Wealth is the ability to fully experience life. (Henry David Thoreau)

Europeans fought for shorter workdays, more vacation time, family leave, and all these kinds of things. Those haven't been priorities in America. It's been about money. You see, in the countries that fought for time, they cook more often, they have less obesity. There are real benefits to having time. (Michael Pollan, American author, journalist, activist)

You aren't wealthy until you have something money can't buy. (Garth Brooks)

That money talks, I'll not deny.
I heard it once. It said, 'Goodbye'. (Richard Armour, 1906-1989, American poet and author)

If you think nobody cares if you're alive, try missing a couple of car payments. (Earl Wilson, 1907-1987, American journalist, gossip columnist, and author)

Money is a new form of slavery, and distinguishable from the old simply by the fact that it is impersonal–that there is no human relation between master and slave.
  (Leo Tolstoy)

If inflation continues to soar, you're going to have to work like a dog just to live like one. (George Gobel, 1919-1991, American comedian)

You don't seem to realize that a poor person who is unhappy is in a better position than a rich person who is unhappy. Because the poor person has hope. He thinks money would help. (Jean Kerr, 1922-2003, Irish-American author and playwright)

The main vice of capitalism is the uneven distribution of prosperity. (Winston Churchill)

Having no debt is to be rich. (Tibetan proverb)

Men pray to the Almighty to relieve poverty. But poverty comes not from God's laws. It is blasphemy of the worst kind to say that. Poverty comes from man's injustice to his fellow man. (Leo Tolstoy)

Never knew how poor I was until I started making money. (Michael Douglas)

I'm tired about hearing about money, money, money, money, money. I just want to play the game, drink Pepsi, wear Reebok. (Shaquille O'Neal)

Being poor means stripping down to the essentials, and there's not much a person really needs to survive-- bread, cheese, blankets, a little black-and-white TV, some toothpaste, soap, pencils, a library card. In and of itself, it isn't bad not to have things, and if all of us lived this way, there would hardly be anything wrong with it at all. To be poor is one thing; to *know* that you are poor is another thing altogether. (Frances Lefkowitz, writer, publisher)

In school, my favorite subject was math. That's where I learned to count money. (French Montana)

A simple fact that is hard to learn is that the time to save money is when you have some. (Joe Moore)

You shouldn't have to have money to have a luxury fragrance. (Lady Gaga)

To get rich, you have to be making money while you're asleep. (David Bailey)

Money and women. They're two of the strongest things in the world. The things you do for a woman you wouldn't do for anything else. Same with money.
  (Satchel Paige)

If you have a gun, you can rob a bank, but if you have a bank, you can rob everyone. (Bill Maher)

You can spend the money on new housing for the poor and the homeless, or you can spend it on a football stadium or a golf course. (Jello Biafra, former lead singer for the San Francisco punk rock band The Dead Kennedys)

If you're in debt, you can't say no. (Tom Hanks)

Do you think that when they asked George Washington for ID that he just whipped out a quarter? (Steven Wright)

100 years ago everyone owned a horse and only the rich had cars. Today everyone has cars and only the rich own horses.

Poverty was the greatest motivating factor in my life. (Jimmy Dean)

When I was young, I used to think that wealth and power would bring me happiness. I was right. (Gahan Wilson)

As the fish sees the bait not the hook, a man sees only the profit, no danger. (Mongolian proverb)

Nobody has been arrested on Wall Street for the crash of 2008. They're not paying their fair share of the taxes. And now with the Citizens United case of the Supreme Court, they get to buy politicians up out in the open. (Michael Moore, 2010)

Affluence creates poverty. (Marshall McLuhan)

People who work sitting down get paid more than people who work standing up. (Ogden Nash)

Success always necessitates a degree of ruthlessness. Given the choice of friendship or success, I'd probably choose success. (Sting)

It is not the employer who pays the wages. Employers only handle the money. It is the customer who pays the wages. (Henry Ford)

I'd like to be rich enough so I could throw soap away after the letters are worn off. (Andy Rooney)

A penny saved is a penny earned. (Benjamin Franklin)

I have too many credit cards. You know what happened? Someone stole one and I didn't notice. I noticed when I got that bill. Whoa! It was so much less! I'm letting him keep it. I'm saving money! (Rita Rudner)

Great desire causes endless poverty. (Indian proverb)

Money doesn't talk, it swears. (Bob Dylan, *It's Alright Ma, I'm Only Bleeding*, 1965)

Rule #1: Never lose money.
Rule #2: Never forget rule #1. (Warren Buffett)

The court is very merciful when the accused is rich. (Hebrew proverb)

Last year people won more than one billion dollars playing poker. And casinos made twenty-seven billion just by being around those people. (Samantha Bee)

Wealthy people miss one of life's great thrills…making the last car payment. (H. Jackson Brown)

Money can't buy poverty. (Marty Feldman)

Son, if you really want something in this life, you have to work for it. Now quiet! They're about to announce the lottery numbers. (Homer Simpson, Matt Groening)

Our money looks like baseball cards with slave owners on it. (Dave Chappelle)

Somebody said to me, 'But the Beatles were anti-materialistic.' That's a huge myth. John and I literally used to sit down and say, 'Now let's write a swimming pool.' (Paul McCartney)

One of the rewards for success is freedom, the ability to do whatever you like. (Sting)

It isn't necessary to be rich and famous to be happy, It's only necessary to be rich. (Alan Alda)

The hardest thing is to take less when you can get more. (Kin Hubbard, American cartoonist, humorist, and journalist)

If a company can't explain, in one sentence, what it does…it's illegal. (Lewis Black)

Wake up, you idiots! Whatever made you think that money was so valuable? (Kurt Vonnegut)

MOVING ON

Time, the subtle thief of youth. (John Milton)

You only live once, but if you do it right, once is enough. (Mae West)

In three words I can sum up everything I've learned about life: it goes on. (Robert Frost)

At my age flowers scare me. (George Burns)

I survived the 60's...twice! (T-shirt)

Fun is like life insurance: the older you get, the more it costs. (Kin Hubbard)

For my sister's 50th birthday, I sent her a singing mammogram. (Steven Wright)

What can I say, I'm old and entitled. (Johnny Ratz)

When you're 20 you care what everyone thinks, when you're 40 you stop caring what everybody thinks, when you're 60 you realize no one was ever thinking about you in the first place. (Winston Churchill)

We are always the same age inside. (Gertrude Stein,1874-1946, American Novelist)

Wisdom doesn't necessarily come with age. Sometimes age just shows up by itself. (Tom Wilson)

A man ninety years old was asked to what he attributed his longevity. 'I reckon,' he said, with a twinkle in his eye, 'it's because most nights I went to bed and slept when I should have sat up and worried.' (Dorothea Kent, 1916-1990, American film actress)

You know how to tell when you're getting old?...When your broad mind changes places with your narrow waist. (Red Skelton)

There's nothing stressful about turning 50 except people reminding you about it. (Mohammad Ali)

Do not worry about avoiding temptation. As you grow older it will avoid you. (Joey Adams)

Growing old is mandatory; growing up is optional. (Chili Davis)

Forty is the old age of youth; fifty the youth of old age. (Victor Hugo)

And what is death, if not a face at peace. It's artistic perfection. (Vladimir Nabokov)

After thirty, a body has a mind of its own. (Bette Midler)

As life goes on it becomes tiring to keep up the character you invented for yourself, and so you relapse into individuality and become more like yourself every day. (Agatha Christie)

I am really looking forward as I get older and older to being less and less nice. (Annette Benning, American actress)

I'm old, I'm young, I'm intelligent, I'm stupid. My tide goes in and out. (Warren Beatty)

Life is really a one-way street, isn't it? (Agatha Christie)

I've found a formula for avoiding these exaggerated fears of age; you take care of every day; let the calendar take care of the years. (Ed Wynn)

When I was a boy the Dead Sea was only sick. (George Burns)

Just remember, once you're over the hill you begin to pick up speed. (Arthur Schopenhauer)

I think of dying every day. At a certain age, you should be prepared to go at any time. (August Wilson)

Rest, nature, books, music…such is my idea of happiness. (Leo Tolstoy)

It's no disgrace to be old. But damn if it isn't inconvenient. (Moms Mabley)

(Speaking of old age) You wake up one morning and you got it. (Moms Mabley)

A person's dying is more his family's affair than his own. (Thomas Mann)

No man goes before his time--unless the boss leaves early. (Groucho Marx)

There's no armored cars in a funeral line. (blues lyric)

Death is no more than passing from one room into another. But there's a difference for me, you know. Because in that other room I shall be able to see. (Helen Keller)

Time is short, life is short, and there's a lot to know. So I skip the entertainers in the newspaper now. I just haven't got time. (Tom Stoppard.)

At the beginning of my shift I placed a stethoscope on an elderly and slightly deaf female patient's anterior chest wall. "Big breaths," I instructed. "Yes, they used to be," sighed the patient. (Dr. Susan Steinberg, from Anna Hamilton's dad)

Every man desires to live long, but no man wishes to be old. (Jonathan Swift)

If you look back on your life and where you started from it's like looking back down a mountain back to the desert floor. It's like now I can't believe I had whatever it takes or perceived whatever it took to get here. (Morgan Freeman)

How do you move on? You move on when your heart finally understands that there is no turning back. (J. R. R. Tolkien)

The last part of life's road has to be walked in single file. (Sri Ramakrishna)

Somebody asked what I wanted on my gravestone. I'm just going to put: 'Glad I could help.' (Dick Van Dyke)

Though a tree grows ever so high, its falling leaves return to the root. (Chinese proverb)

Those who love deeply never grow old. They may die of old age, but they die young. (Dorothy Canfield Fisher)

To die is easy. To live with dignity is hard. (Japanese proverb)

Go to Heaven for the climate, Hell for the company. (Mark Twain)

Your character is your destiny. (Tibetan proverb)

We're born alone, we live alone, we die alone. Only through our love and friendship can we create the illusion for the moment that we're not alone. (Orson Welles)

Old birds are hard to pluck. (German proverb)

If you believe you are in control of your life, steering it in a course of your choosing, then old age is an affront, because it is a destination you didn't choose. But if you think of life instead as an improvisation in response to the stream of events coming at you—that is, as a response to the world as it is—then old age is more another chapter in a long-running story. The events are different, but they're always different. (John Leland, Metro reporter for *The New York Times*)

Immortality would probably get frustrating after a while. (Kieran Setiya)

We must let go of the life we have planned, so as to accept the one that is waiting for us. (Joseph Campbell)

Drown in a cold vat of whiskey? Death, where is thy sting? (W. C. Fields)

What you really value is what you miss, not what you have. (Jorge Luis Borges)

My uncle's dying wish: he wanted me on his lap. He was in the electric chair. (Rodney Dangerfield)

My earrings are worth just enough to buy me a coffin if I die in a strange place. That was the reason why sailors used to wear them. (Morgan Freeman)

As a well-spent day brings happy sleep, so a life well spent brings happy death. (Leonardo da Vinci)

I'm the oldest antique in town. (Norman Rockwell)

If I had to live my life over, I'd live over a saloon. (W. C. Fields)

The secret of staying young is to live honestly, eat slowly, and lie about your age. (Lucille Ball)

People living deeply have no fear of death. (Anais Nin)

My husband wanted to be cremated. I told him I'd scatter his ashes at Neiman Marcus--that way, I'd visit him every day. (Joan Rivers)

Life well spent is long. (Leonardo da Vinci)

I was thinking about how people seem to read the Bible a whole lot more as they get older; then it dawned on me...they're cramming for their final exam. (George Carlin)

They say we die twice—once when the last breath leaves our body and once when the last person we know says our name. (Al Pacino)

As you get older three things happen: The first is your memory goes, and I can't remember the other two.
  (Norman Wisdom,1915-2010, English actor, comedian)

Just beat my record for most consecutive days without dying. (Bill Murray)

If any of you cry at my funeral I'll never speak to you again. (Stan Laurel)

I thought growing old would take longer. (T-shirt)

Life is a near-death experience. (George Carlin)

The really frightening thing about middle age is the knowledge that you'll grow out of it. (Doris Day)

Most of my time is spent trying to turn into an old man gracefully. But fortunately, I am very immature for my age. (Mike Bethard)

When an old person dies, a library is lost. (Tommy Swann)

My personal telephone book is a book of the dead now. I'm so old. Almost all of my friends have died, and I don't have the guts to take their names out of the book. (Ray Bradbury)

Getting old is like climbing a mountain; you get a little out of breath, but the view is much better! (Ingrid Bergman)

Did you just call me old? I really prefer the word 'experienced.' (Morgan Freeman)

When I die, if the word 'thong' appears in the first or second sentence of my obituary, I've screwed up. (Albert Brooks)

I'm not exactly a Zen Buddhist. I'm just old, which is almost the same thing. (Sparrow)

The older the grapes, the sweeter the wine. (Janis Joplin)

Perhaps we don't need these religious concoctions to pillow the fear of death. Just the fact that there is an unknown, and something greater, can bring a feeling of peace. That's enough for me. (Brad Pitt)

Dying is the privilege of the weary. (Edgard Varese, 1883-1965, French/American composer)

Don't cry because it's over; smile because it happened.
  (Dr. Seuss)

I want to go and go, and then drop dead in the middle of something I'm loving to do. And if that doesn't happen, if I wind up sitting in a wheelchair, at least I'll have my high heels on. (Dolly Parton)

I love the smell of juice boxes in the morning. (Robert Duvall)

Every time a good child dies, an angel of God comes down to earth. He takes the child in his arms, spreads out his great white wings, and flies with it all over the places the child loved on earth. The angel plucks a large handful of flowers, and they carry it with them up to God, where the flowers bloom more brightly than they ever did on earth. (Hans Christian Andersen)

Come grow old with me, for the best is yet to come.
  (Robert Frost)

I hate funerals. They aren't for the guy who's dead. They're for the guys who are left alive and enjoy mourning. (Humphrey Bogart)

Death may be the greatest of all human blessings.
  (Socrates)

According to one story of his last words, Voltaire's response to a priest at his deathbed urging him to denounce Satan was "Now is not the time for making new enemies."

Youth has no age. (Pablo Picasso)

Rolling along…then napping…that's my motto! (Jodi Siegel)

If I should die, God forbid, let this be my epitaph: "The only proof he needed for the existence of God was music." (Kurt Vonnegut)

For they had lived together long enough to know that love was always love, anytime and anyplace, but it was more solid the closer it came to death. (Gabriel Garcia Marquez)

I get up in the morning and read the obituary column. If I'm not there I go make coffee. (George Burns)

Thank God there's a Jedi pension plan! (Mark Hamill on portraying Luke Skywalker for over 40 years, *AARP Magazine*)

If there comes a day when we can't be together,
Keep me in your heart, and I'll stay there forever. (A.A. Milne)

No need to hurry. No need to sparkle. No need to be anybody but oneself. (Virginia Woolf)

Enjoy life. There's plenty of time to be dead. (Hans Christian Andersen)

OPTIMISM

You've got to *Accentuate the Positive*
Eliminate the negative
Latch on to the affirmative
Don't mess with Mister In-Between
  (Johnny Mercer, song lyric, 1944)

Part of being optimistic is keeping one's head pointed towards the sun, one's feet moving forward. (Nelson Mandala)

Every strike brings me closer to the next home run.
  (Babe Ruth)

Choose to be optimistic. It feels better. (Dalai Lama)

I never get tired of the blue sky. (Vincent van Gogh)

"What day is it?" asked Pooh.
"It's today," squeaked Piglet.
"My favorite day," said Pooh. (A. A. Milne)

In spite of everything I still believe that people are really good at heart. (Anne Frank)

There is something in the human spirit that will survive and prevail, there is a tiny and brilliant light burning in the heart of man that will not go out no matter how dark the world becomes. (Leo Tolstoy)

I, not events, have the power to make me happy or unhappy today. I can choose which it shall be. Yesterday is dead, tomorrow hasn't arrived yet. I have just one day, today, and I'm going to be happy in it. (Groucho Marx)

Some goals are so worthy, it's glorious even to fail.

116

The whole world is a series of miracles, but we're so used to them we call them ordinary things. (Hans Christian Andersen)

Problems are opportunities in work clothes. (Henry Kaiser)

You've got to think lucky. If you fall into a mud hole, check your back pocket...you might have caught a fish. (Darrell Royal, 1924-2012, American football player and coach)

We are the ones we've been waiting for. (June Jordan, 1936-2002, Caribbean-American poet, essayist, teacher, and activist)

Cool, logical, big-eared and level-headed, the center of Star Trek's optimistic, inclusive vision of humanity's future. I loved Spock. (Barack Obama)

Failure is success if we learn from it. (Malcomb S. Forbes)

I have learned from my mistakes, and I am sure I can repeat them exactly. (Peter Cook)

May your choices reflect your hopes, not your fears. (Nelson Mandela)

A pessimist sees the difficulty in every opportunity; an optimist sees the opportunity in every difficulty. (Winston Churchill)

If you are feeling overly optimistic the Republican Candidates Debate is on. (Kristen Schaal, American actress, comedian, writer)

Perpetual optimism is a force multiplier. (Colin Powell)

I always like to look on the optimistic side of life. (Walt Disney)

I don't like that man. I must get to know him better. (Abraham Lincoln)

Being an optimist after you've got everything you want doesn't count. (Kin Hubbard, 1868-1930, American cartoonist, humorist, and journalist)

All things seem possible in May. (Edwin Way Teale)

Grab your coat and get your hat
Leave your worry on the doorstep
Just direct your feet
To the *Sunny Side of the Street.*
  (Dorothy Fields, song lyric, 1930)

PARENTS

If I ever had twins, I'd use one for parts. (Steven Wright)

The thing about kids is they express emotion. They don't hold back. If they want to cry, they cry, and if they're in a good mood, they're in a good mood. (Eddie Murphy)

Never ask your children if they need money. (Dave Cross)

I was so naïve as a kid I used to sneak behind the barn and do nothing. (Johnny Carson)

A loving heart maintains a family; a hateful heart destroys it.

It's so easy for a kid to join a gang, to do drugs. We should make it that easy to be involved in football and academics. (Snoop Dog)

We are most nearly ourselves when we achieve the seriousness of the child at play. (Heraclitus, Greek philosopher, c. 500 B.C.)

I am probably responsible for the odd fact that people don't seem to name their daughters Lolita any more. I have heard of young female poodles being given that name since 1958, but of no human beings. (Vladimir Nabokov)

Sweater: n., garment worn by a child when their mother is feeling chilly. (Ambrose Bierce)

Right now, all over the country, teenage girls are waking up to newsfeeds full of posts written by adults in their lives that say teenage boys attempting to rape them is "just how boys are" and "they can't help themselves" and "they grow out of it" and "it was just a little harmless fun." Think. Think about what that must be doing to them. And when you are done thinking about that, imagine all the teenage boys reading the same thing. (Ashley Garrett, Multimedia Journalist)

I'm terrified of growing up. Once you become an adult, how do you step back from that? It's something that wakes me up at night. (Lorde)

I got a lot of support from my parents. That's the one thing I always appreciated. They didn't tell me I was being stupid, they told me I was being funny. (Jim Carrey)

I wanna make a jigsaw puzzle that's 40,000 pieces. And when you finish it, it says, 'Go outside.' (Demetri Martin, American comedian)

One of the luckiest things that can happen to you in life is, I think, to have a happy childhood. (Agatha Christie)

Never loan your car to anyone to whom you have given birth. (Erma Bombeck)

Now the thing about having a baby--and I can't be the first person to have noticed this--is that thereafter you have it. (Jean Kerr)

Everyone should have kids. They are the greatest joy in the world. But they are also terrorists. You'll realize this as soon as they are born, and they start using sleep deprivation to break you. (Ray Romano)

Nothing beats watching your children become smarter and cooler than you are. (Barack Obama)

Do not confine your children to your own learning, for they were born in another time. (Hebrew proverb)

Adulthood is overrated, maturity is underrated. (Mike D, of the Beastie Boys)

When I was born I was so ugly the doctor slapped my mother. (Rodney Dangerfield)

Your child is never not your child. You can be 90 and your mother 120, but your mother is still worried about you. (Joan Rivers)

Any kid will run an errand for you, if you ask at bedtime. (Red Skelton)

Woman understands children better than man does, but man is more childlike than woman. (Frederic Nietzsche)

We are constantly being surprised that people did things well before we were born. (Robert Benchley)

I'm not a role model. Just because I dunk a basketball doesn't mean I should raise your kids. (Charles Barkley)

The father of a daughter is nothing but a high-class hostage. A father turns a stony face to his sons, berates them, shakes his antlers, paws the ground, snorts, runs them off into the underbrush, but when his daughter puts her arm over his shoulder and says, 'Daddy, I need to ask you something,' he is a pat of butter in a hot frying pan. (Garrison Keillor)

BOY: n., noise with dirt on it. (T-shirt)

When I was a kid my parents moved a lot, but I always found them. (Rodney Dangerfield)

121

No matter what, your parents are going to worry about you. I had a tour bus, and my mother still thought I was broke. (Lewis Black)

Hello babies: Welcome to Earth. It's hot in the summer and cold in the winter. It's round and wet and crowded. At the outside, babies, you've got about a hundred years here. There's only one rule that I know of, babies: God damn it, you've got to be kind. (Kurt Vonnegut)

The hardest job kids face today is learning good manners without seeing any. (Fred Astaire)

Adults are obsolete children. (Dr. Seuss)

I was kind of a strange child. My parents knew early on that something must have been wrong with me. I crawled backwards until I was two, but had Kennedy's inaugural address memorized by the time I was six. (Michael Moore)

If love alone could cure our children, they would always be well. (Debbie Reynolds)

I think, at a child's birth, if a mother could ask a fairy godmother to endow it with the most useful gift, that gift should be curiosity. (Eleanor Roosevelt)

Parents have got to chill out. Let your kid eat dirt. They're gonna be fine. (Jeff Garlin, American comedian, actor, producer, director, and writer)

Everybody's family has different values. (Lewis Black)

As a small child, I felt in my heart two contradictory feelings, the horror of life and the ecstasy of life. (Charles Baudelaire)

How many teenagers does it take to screw in a lightbulb?...Whatever.

Cleaning your house while your kids are still growing up is like shoveling the walk before it stops snowing.
  (Phyllis Diller)

Mom and Pop were just a couple of kids when they got married. He was eighteen, she was sixteen and I was three. (Billie Holiday)

Kids should be allowed to break stuff more often. That's a consequence of exploration. Exploration is what you do when you don't know what you're doing. (Neil deGrasse Tyson)

An ant colony is every bit as complex and organized as human society. If fact, it is more organized, because there are no teenagers. (Dave Barry, American author and columnist)

My standard comment is, 'If you don't want your kids to be like Bart Simpson, don't act like Homer Simpson.'
  (Matt Groening)

Be who you needed when you were younger. (Gas station sandwich board)

My mother and father were never frightened of anything. They always felt that they should go through life happily and without fear, and they did that. And it was a great boon to my brother and myself. (John Cassavetes)

I have good looking kids. Luckily, my wife cheats on me.
  (Rodney Dangerfield)

When I was young, an eccentric uncle decided to teach me how to lie. Not, he explained, because he wanted me

123

to lie, but because I should know how it's done so I would recognize when I was being lied to. (Brian Eno)

Children learn to smile from their parents. (Shinichi Suzuki, Japanese musician, philosopher, and educator)

What I always want to tell young people now is: Pay attention. This isn't gonna happen again. (Carrie Fisher)

A newlywed talking to her friend who has children: 'What if I have a child and I dedicate my life to it and it grows up and hates me, and it blames everything that's wrong with its life on me,' and my friend replied, 'Don't be silly, what do you mean, What if?' (Rita Rudner)

A father is a banker provided by nature. (French proverb)

Having one child makes you a parent; having two, you are a referee. (David Frost)

A mother takes twenty years to make a man of her boy, and another woman makes of fool of him in twenty minutes. (Robert Frost)

Music rhythms are mathematical patterns. When you hear a song and your body starts moving with it, your body is doing math. The kids in their parents' garage practicing to be a band may not realize it, but they're also practicing math. (Kareem Abdul-Jabbar)

It stands to reason that unloved and unwanted children are going to get into crime. (Andrew Young)

I don't even know how to speak up for myself, because I don't really have a father who would give me the confidence or advice. (Eminem)

I'm gonna put a curse on you and all your kids will be born completely naked. (Jimi Hendrix)

Remember this: It's your life, not theirs. Just because your parents sent you to college doesn't mean they bought the rest of your life. (Lewis Black)

If evolution really works, how come mothers only have two hands? (Milton Berle)

With every word we utter, with every action we take, we know our kids are watching us. We as parents are their most important role models. (Michelle Obama)

Wrinkles are hereditary. Parents get them from their children. (Doris Day)

PARTNERS

Love one another and you will be happy. It's as simple and as difficult as that. (Michael Leunig, Australian artist & cartoonist)

My husband says I look like a Q-tip. (Dolly Parton)

You don't love someone for their looks, or their clothes, or for their fancy car, but because they sing a song only you can hear. (Oscar Wilde)

Only married people understand you can be miserable and happy at the same time. (Chris Rock)

I don't like to discuss my marriage, but I will tell you something which may sound corny but which happens to be true. I have steak at home. Why should I go out for a hamburger? (Paul Newman)

Politics doesn't make strange bedfellows--marriage does. (Groucho Marx)

We would have broken up except for the children. Who were the children? Well, she and I were. (Mort Saul)

They say marriages are made in Heaven. But so is thunder and lightning. (Clint Eastwood)

An archaeologist is the best husband a woman can have. The older she gets the more interested he is in her. (Agatha Christie)

I like marriage. The idea. (Toni Morrison)

I hope that when I'm 80 years old, people will still be talking about my wedding. (Jennifer Hudson, American singer and actress)

The best romance is inside marriage, the finest love stories come after the wedding, not before. (Irving Stone)

I was blessed that I got married early and had a good wife. That sort of kept me straight. Probably I would have been like Charlie Parker, you know, involved in drugs or alcohol or something like that if I hadn't had this stability. (Dizzy Gillespie)

My wife and I were happy for twenty years…then we met. (Rodney Dangerfield)

A successful marriage requires falling in love many times, always with the same person. (Mignon McLaughlin)

The male is a domestic animal which, if treated with firmness and kindness, can be trained to do most things. (Jilly Cooper, English author)

Each friend represents a world in us, a world not born until they arrive, and it is only by this meeting that a new world is born. (Anais Nin)

Remember that the most valuable antiques are dear old friends. (H. Jackson Brown, Jr.)

My wife wants sex in the back seat of the car and she wants me to drive. (Rodney Dangerfield)

If we were all given by magic the power to read each other's thoughts, I suppose the first effect would be to dissolve all friendships. (Bertrand Russell)

There is nothing on this earth more to be prized than true friendship. (Thomas Aquinas)

I haven't spoken to my wife in years. I didn't want to interrupt her. (Rodney Dangerfield)

The real friend tells you the bitter truth.

Be brave, young lovers, and follow your star. (Oscar Hammerstein, *The King and I,* 1951)

At the end of the day, if the guy is going to write the girl a letter, whether it's chicken scratch or scribble or looks like a doctor's note, if he takes the time to put pen to paper and not type something, there's something so incredibly romantic and beautiful about that. (Meghan Markle)

There is only one happiness in this life, to love and be loved. (George Sand)

Of all possessions a friend is the most precious. (Herodotus)

A man doesn't know what happiness is until he's married. By then, it's too late. (Frank Sinatra)

Friends show their love in times of trouble, not in happiness. (Euripides)

It's a funny thing that when a man hasn't anything on earth to worry about, he goes off and gets married. (Robert Frost)

A man would prefer to come home to an unmade bed and a happy woman than a neatly made bed and an angry woman. (Marlene Dietrich)

When you realize you want to spend the rest of your life with somebody, you want the rest of your life to start as soon as possible. (Nora Ephron, *When Harry Met Sally*, 1989)

I blame my mother for my poor sex life. All she told me was 'the man goes on top and the woman underneath.' For three years my husband and I slept in bunk beds. (Joan Rivers)

Some people care too much. I think it's called love. (A. A. Milne)

By all means marry; if you get a good wife, you'll become happy; if you get a bad one, you'll become a philosopher. (Socrates)

I love you, and because I love you I would sooner have you hate me for telling you the truth than adore me for telling you lies. (Pietro Aretino, 1492-1556, Italian author, playwright, poet)

Of all the home remedies, a good wife is best. (Kin Hubbard)

When my love swears that she is made of truth,
I do believe her, though I know she lies,
That she might think me some untutored youth,
Unlearnèd in the world's false subtleties.
Thus vainly thinking that she thinks me young,
Although she knows my days are past the best,
Simply I credit her false-speaking tongue:
On both sides thus is simple truth suppressed.
But wherefore says she not she is unjust?
And wherefore say not I that I am old?
Oh, love's best habit is in seeming trust,
And age in love loves not to have years told.
   Therefore I lie with her and she with me,
   And in our faults by lies we flattered be.
     (William Shakespeare, 1564-1616, Sonnet 138)

Researchers in Canada say they have discovered the part of a man's brain that is used to make decisions, and this is weird: it's actually located in your wife's brain.
 (Jimmy Fallon)

I always cry at weddings, especially my own. (Humphrey Bogart)

Hurt me with the truth, don't comfort me with a lie.
 (Rihanna)

A kiss is like singing into someone's mouth. (Diane Ackerman)

Happy domestic life is like a beautiful summer's evening; the heart is filled with peace, and everything around derives a peculiar glory. (Hans Christian Andersen)

It's not that we don't get along, it's just that my mother-in-law is very objective. She objected to everything I did.
 (Beverly D'Angelo, American actress and singer)

People stay married because they want to, not because the doors are locked.
 (Paul Newman)

1st man: My wife treats me like I'm God.
2nd man: So she worships, honors and obeys you?
1st man: No, she ignores me until she wants something.

It was so cold the other day, I almost got married.
(Shelley Winters)

PEP TALK

The key to success in life is using the good thoughts of wise people. (Leo Tolstoy)

If you do not change direction, you may end up where you are heading. (Lao Tzu)

I felt like they wanted me to fail and I thought, I'm not going to go anywhere. I'm going to get my glory. I'm going to get my shine. (Iggy Azalea)

Never be afraid to sit awhile and think. (Lorraine Hansberry, 1930-1965, African-American playwright and writer,)

Act as if you are, and you will become such. (Leo Tolstoy)

GODIDIT (CA license plate)

The secret of getting ahead is getting started. (Mark Twain)

Don't let what you cannot do interfere with what you can do. (John Wooden, USC basketball coach)

The doer alone learneth. (Friedrich Nietzsche)

The best way to make your dreams come true is to wake up. (Paul Valery)

Don't be pushed by your problems. Be led by your dreams. (Ralph Waldo Emerson)

Keep your eyes on the stars, and your feet on the ground. (Theodore Roosevelt)

Focus more on your desire than on your doubt, and the dream will take of itself. (Mark Twain)

Success consists of going from failure to failure without loss of enthusiasm. (Winston Churchill)

To achieve great things, two things are needed: a plan, and not quite enough time. (Leonard Bernstein)

Some say talent is energy and that's a very interesting way of thinking about it. In other words, people with talent have a lot of energy. (Annette Benning)

Do not be too moral. You may cheat yourself out of much life so. (Henry David Thoreau)

A lion sleeps in the heart of every brave man. (Turkish proverb)

One of the things I learned the hard way was that it doesn't pay to get discouraged. Keeping busy and making optimism a way of life can restore your faith in yourself. (Lucille Ball)

Genius is eternal patience. (Michelangelo)

If a man does not keep pace with his companions,
Perhaps it is because he hears a different drummer.
Let him step to the music which he hears,
However measured or far away. (Henry David Thoreau)

Dreams don't have a deadline. (LLCoolJ)

We're stronger in the places that we've been broken.
  (Ernest Hemingway)

You have to sniff out joy, keep your nose to the joy-trail.
  (Buffy Sainte-Marie)

Always dream and shoot higher than you know you can do. Do not bother just to be better than your contemporaries or predecessors. Try to be better than yourself. (William Faulkner)

Pleasures are transient, honors are immortal. (Greek proverb)

Never confuse the size of your paycheck with the size of your talent. (Marlon Brando)

I'm a survivor. A living example of what people can go through and survive. (Elizabeth Taylor)

Failure is the condiment that gives success its flavor. (Truman Capote)

The difference between a hero and a coward is the direction in which they run. (Mongolian proverb)

There are two kinds of truth: the truth that lights the way and the truth that warms the heart. The first of these is science, and the second is art. (Raymond Chandler)

Patience is also a form of action. (Auguste Rodin)

The best way to guarantee a loss is to quit. (Morgan Freeman)

Do what you love. Know your own bone; gnaw at it, bury it, unearth it, and gnaw it still. (Henry David Thoreau)

Things are never so bad they can't be made worse. (Humphrey Bogart)

Fear is a reaction. Courage is a decision. (Winston Churchill)

Every obstacle yields to stern resolve. (Leonardo da Vinci)

I love my rejection slips. They show me I try. (Sylvia Plath)

The souls that have seen the darkest days can shine the brightest light. Keep going! (Heidi Stea)

It is easy to hate and it is difficult to love. This is how the whole scheme of things works. All good things are difficult to achieve; and bad things are easy to get. (Confucius)

Freedom lies in being bold. (Robert Frost)

Our greatest weakness lies in giving up. The most certain way to succeed is always to try just one more time. (Thomas A. Edison)

Turn your wounds into wisdom. (Oprah Winfrey)

I never had one beer. If I bought a six-pack of beer, I kept drinking 'til all six beers were gone. You have to have that kind of understanding about yourself. I haven't had a drink now in 12 years. (Samuel L. Jackson)

You don't have to be the biggest to beat the biggest. (Ross Perot)

An exciting new phase in your life is about to begin. Secrete abdominal fluids to soften the inside of your cocoon and fly out. (Tom Newbill)

If your ship doesn't come in, swim out to it. (Jonathan Winters)

A diamond is a chunk of coal that made good under pressure.

I was the shyest human ever invented, but I had a lion inside me that wouldn't shut up! (Ingrid Bergman)

The third-rate mind is only happy when it is thinking with the majority. The second-rate mind is only happy when it is thinking with the minority. The first-rate mind is only happy when it is thinking. (A. A. Milne)

I periodically realize every few years that the person whose taste I really trust is me. (Brian Eno)

Silence is a true friend. (Confucius)

I never dwell on what happened. You can't change it. Move forward. Don't waste your energy on being angry at something that somebody did six months ago or a year ago. It's over. Done. Move forward. (Joan Rivers)

Behold the turtle. He makes progress only when he sticks his neck out. (James B. Conant, 1893-1978, American chemist, President of Harvard University)

They can conquer who believe they can. (Virgil)

Don't be afraid to see what you see. (Ronald Reagan)

When you are face to face with a difficulty, you are up against discovery. (William Thomson, 1824-1907, Scotch-Irish mathematical physicist and engineer)

It does not matter how slowly you go as long as you do not stop. (Confucius)

Don't be seduced into thinking that that which does not make a profit is without value. (Arthur Williams)

Well begun is half done. (Aristotle)

Getting sausage is a great deal like life. You get out of it what you put into it. (Jimmy Dean)

Faith in oneself is the best and safest course. (Michelangelo)

By three methods we learn wisdom: First, by reflection. which is noblest; second, by imitation, which is easiest; and third, by experience, which is the bitterest. (Confucius)

There is never a wrong time to do the right thing. (H. Jackson Brown)

A positive thinker sees the invisible, feels the intangible, and achieves the impossible. (Winston Churchill)

Start where you are. Use what you have. Do what you can. (Arthur Ashe)

Life is now. (Oprah Winfrey)

Be so good they can't ignore you. (Steve Martin)

POETRY

Star light, star bright
First star I see tonight
Wish I may, wish I might
Have the wish I wish tonight
   (English nursery rhyme)

To see a World in a Grain of Sand
And a Heaven in a Wild Flower
Hold Infinity in the palm of your hand
And Eternity in an hour
   From *Auguries of Innocence* (William Blake)

Here lies Matthew Mudd,
Death did him no hurt;
When alive he was only Mudd,
But now he's only dirt.
   (Mel Blanc)

...everywhere
The ceremony of innocence is drowned;
The best lack all conviction, while the worst
Are full of passionate intensity:
...what rough beast, its hour come round at last,
Slouches towards Bethlehem to be born?
   From *The Second Coming* (William Butler Yeats)

Never send to know for whom the bell tolls;
It tolls for thee. (John Donne)

I wish our clever young poets would remember my
homely definitions of prose and poetry: prose = words in
their best order; poetry = the best words in the best
order. (Samuel Taylor Coleridge)

Poetry is indispensable. If only I knew what for. (Jean
Cocteau)

From there to here
And here to there
Funny things are everywhere. (Dr. Seuss)

I consider myself a poet first and a musician second. I
live like a poet and I'll die like a poet. (Bob Dylan)

I love poetry. I love rhyming. Do you know, there are
poets who don't rhyme? Shakespeare did not rhyme
most of the time, and that's why I do not like him. (Chuck
Berry)

I was reading the dictionary. I thought it was a poem
about everything. (Steven Wright)

Poetry is the synthesis of hyacinths and biscuits. (Carl
Sandburg)

One impulse from a vernal wood
May teach you more of man,
Of moral evil and of good
Than all the sages can.
   (William Wordsworth)

I would be married, but I'd have no wife,
I would be married to a single life.
   (Charles Bukowski)

Come live with me and be my love,
And we will all the pleasures prove,
That valleys, groves, hills, and fields,
Woods, or steepy mountain yields.
   (Christopher Marlowe)

Every day, my daddy told me the same thing:
'Once a task is just begun, never leave it till it's done.
Be the labour great or small, do it well or not at all.'
   (Quincy Jones)

Democracy don't rule the world,
You'd better get that in your head;
This world is ruled by violence,
But I guess that's better left unsaid.
   (Bob Dylan, *Union Sundown*, 1983)

And Priests in black gowns, were walking their rounds,
And binding with briars, my joys & desires.
   (William Blake)

A truth that's told with bad intent
Beats all the lies you can invent.
   (William Blake)

The storm starts, when the drops start dropping.
When the drops stop dropping then the storm starts
stopping.
   (Dr. Seuss)

His labor is a chant
   His idleness a tune
Oh, for a bee's experience
   Of clovers, and of noon.
   (Emily Dickenson)

Poetry is an echo, asking a shadow to dance. (Carl
Sandburg)

Today you are you,
   that is truer than true.
There is no one alive
   that is youer than you.
   (Dr. Seuss)

God made boys from a piece of string
   He had some left over so He left a little thing
God made girls from a piece of lace

He didn't have enough so He left a little place
Thank you, God.

POLITICS & HISTORY

Elect a clown, expect a circus. (T-shirt)

We need more people speaking out. This country is not overrun with rebels and free thinkers. It's overrun with sheep and conformists. (Bill Maher)

When in doubt, mumble;
When in trouble, delegate;
When in charge, ponder. (James H Boren, 1925–2010, American humorist and writer)

Democracy continues with or without you. (Michelle Obama)

When you talk about the future the devil laughs. (Japanese proverb)

January, 2028: President Standing Bear signs an executive order to deport all Caucasians back to Europe.

The charm of history and its enigmatic lesson consist in the fact that, from age to age, nothing changes and yet everything is completely different. (Aldous Huxley)

Tolerance of intolerance is cowardice. (Ayaan Hirsi Ali, Somali-born Dutch-American activist, feminist, author)

Washington is dominated by big money. (Bernie Sanders)

The way to study the past is not to confine oneself to a mere knowledge of history but, through application of this knowledge, to give actuality to the past. (Sri Ramakrishna)

The way my luck is running, if I was a politician I would be honest. (Rodney Dangerfield)

What is history after all? History is facts which become lies in the end. (Jean Cocteau, 1889-1963, French writer and filmmaker)

When I first ran for Congress, I went to my daughter Alexandra, who was going to be a senior in high school, and said: 'I have a chance to run. I may not win, but I'd be gone three nights a week. So, if you want me to stay, I'll be happy to.' And do you know what she said to me? 'Mother, get a life!' (Nancy Pelosi)

God cannot alter the past, but historians can. (Samuel Butler)

The game of history is usually played by the best and the worst over the heads of the majority in the middle. (Eric Hoffer)

Never interrupt your enemy when he's making a mistake. (Napoleon Bonaparte)

Perhaps in time the so-called dark ages will be thought of as including our own. (Georg Christoph Lichtenberg, 1742-1799, German physicist and satirist)

Blood alone moves the wheels of history. (Martin Luther)

I voted in every election--not always for the same political party and never with any degree of enthusiasm. (Tom Stoppard)

Historians are like deaf people who go on answering questions that no one has asked them. (Leo Tolstoy)

A peasant between two lawyers is like a fish between two cats. (Spanish proverb)

The "*duck* test" is a form of abductive reasoning. This is its usual expression: *If* it looks *like a duck*, swims *like a duck*, and quacks *like a duck*, then it probably is a *duck*.

Either all people are created equal--or they're not. You're either buying into the original premise of America--or you're not. (Jon Stewart)

Political language--and with variations this is true of all political parties, from Conservatives to Anarchists--is designed to make lies sound truthful and murder sound respectable, and to give an appearance of solidity to pure wind. (George Orwell)

The constitutional freedom of religion is the most inalienable and sacred of all human rights. (Thomas Jefferson)

Religion is regarded by the common people as true, by the wise as false, and by the rulers as useful. (Seneca, 4 B.C.-65 A.D., Roman philosopher)

Few people are capable of expressing with equanimity opinions which differ from the prejudices of their social environment. Most people are even incapable of forming such opinions. (Albert Einstein)

One of the key problems today is that politics is such a disgrace, people don't go into government. (Donald Trump)

I debated in high school! If you told things that weren't true or just made things out of whole cloth, you were penalized. It's too bad they don't apply the same standards to presidential candidates as they do to high school students. (Mark Hamill, Luke Skywalker, *Star Wars*)

Nixon is one of the few in the history of this country to run for high office talking out of both sides of his mouth at the same time and lying out of both sides.

Capitalism means that a few people will do very well, and the rest will serve the few. (Michael Moore)

There is nothing so stable as change. (Bob Dylan)

Three percent of the population now owns half of the country's firearms. These are men who are anxious about their ability to protect their families, insecure about their place in the job market, and beset by racial fears. They tend to be less educated, a population that is struggling to find a new story—one in which they are once again the heroes. Stockpiling guns seems to be a symptom of a much deeper crisis in meaning and purpose in their lives. (Injury Control Research Center at Harvard University)

Giving money and power to government is like giving whiskey and car keys to teenage boys. (P. J. O'Rourke)

Nothing strengthens authority so much as silence. (Leonardo da Vinci)

I contend that for a nation to try to tax itself into prosperity is like a man standing in a bucket and trying to lift himself up by the handle. (Mark Twain)

A unionized public employee, a member of the Tea Party, and a CEO are sitting at a table. In the middle of the table is a plate with a dozen cookies on it. The CEO reaches across and takes eleven of the cookies, looks at the Tea Partier, and says, "Look out for that union guy. He wants a piece of your cookie." (*Sun* magazine)

The nine most terrifying words in the English language are: 'I'm from the government and I'm here to help.' (Ronald Reagan)

Of all dangers to a nation, as things exist in our day, there can be no greater one than having certain portions of the people set off from the rest by a line drawn--they not privileged as others, but degraded, humiliated, made of no account. (Walt Whitman)

Laws are the great riverbanks between which society flows. The law verbalizes aggression, taming it through an adversarial system that requires each party to listen to the other's argument. (Yale Law School Dean, quoted in Wilkinson, *All Falling Faiths*)

BLUSTAT (California License Plate)

Politics is the art of looking for trouble, finding it everywhere, diagnosing it incorrectly and applying the wrong remedies. (Groucho Marx)

I hate the press. But the fact is we need a free press. We must have it. It's vital; if you want to preserve democracy as we know it, you have to have a free and many times adversarial press. Without it, I am afraid that we would lose much of our individual liberties over time. That's how dictators get started. When you look at history, the first thing that dictators do is shut down the press. (John McCain)

The death of one man is a tragedy but the death of a million is a statistic. (Joseph Stalin)

The genius of Einstein leads to Hiroshima. (Pablo Picasso)

If we don't figure out as collective human beings how to get along with each other, even the people we don't like and with whom we don't agree--say the Americans and the Russians, the Americans and the Chinese, the Americans and anybody else--if we don't figure out collectively how to get along with each other and take care of each other, that might be the end of humanity. (Jimmy Carter)

I imagine most of that stuff on the information highway is roadkill anyway. (John Updike)

There is no idea so foolish but that it cannot be put into the heads of an ignorant and incapable multitude, especially if the idea holds out some prospect of any gain or advantage. (Arthur Schopenhauer)

The further a society drifts from the truth, the more it will hate those who speak it. (George Orwell)

Politics: The conduct of public affairs for private advantage. (Ambrose Bierce)

You have enemies? Good. That means you stood up for something. (Winston Churchill)

Diplomacy is the art of telling people to go to hell in such a way that they ask for directions. (Winston Churchill)

One man with conviction will overwhelm a hundred who only have opinions. (Winston Churchill)

Everyone is in favor of free speech. Hardly a day passes without its being extolled, but some people's idea of it is that they are free to say what they like, but if anyone

146

else says anything back, that is an outrage. (Winston Churchill)

Socialism appeals to me. It's like imposed Christianity. You've got to share. (Lewis Black)

I'm a happy person but an angry citizen. (Lewis Black)

If a group of people, leaders, can convince a group of folk who barely have a pot to piss in that the rich shouldn't be taxed, THAT is leadership! (Lewis Black)

I was friends with President Ronald Reagan and he once said to me, 'I don't know how anybody can serve in public office without being an actor.' (Warren Beatty)

The success of the union movement, historically, has always been to benefit all working men and women--not just people who belong to the union. (Warren Beatty)

My definition of redundancy is an air-bag in a politician's car. (Larry Hagman, 1931-2012, American film and television actor, director and producer)

I think to each his own. If nobody is hurting anybody-- who cares? Everybody should be able to do what they want and be happy. Who you love is who you love. That's the way I see it. (Jennifer Hudson)

One picture is worth 1,000 denials. (Ronald Reagan)

I believe that order is better than chaos, creation better than destruction. I prefer gentleness to violence, forgiveness to vendetta. On the whole I think knowledge is preferable to ignorance, and I am sure human sympathy is more valuable than ideology. (Leo Tolstoy)

The Four Stages of Idealism:
  1) Your head in the clouds
  2) Your head in the sand
  3) Your head up your ass
  4) Your head on a plate

The Republicans do not have feelings for people who
are in bad shape. (Joy Behar)

I just want to say something. 655,000 Iraqi civilians are
dead. Who are the terrorists? (Rosie O'Donnell)

I prefer the most unjust peace to the most righteous war.
  (Cicero)

To save your world you asked this man to die;
Would this man, could he see you now, ask why? (W.H.
Auden)

Alliance: In international politics, the union of two thieves
who have their hands so deeply inserted into each
other's' pockets that they cannot separately plunder a
third. (Ambrose Bierce)

When you've seen one nuclear war, you've seen them
all.

Violence is not power, but the absence of power. (Ralph
Waldo Emerson)

War is not nice. (Barbara Bush)

There is one thing stronger than all the armies in the
world, and that is an idea whose time has come. (Victor
Hugo)

Politics is more difficult than physics. (Albert Einstein)

The Statue of Liberty is no longer saying, 'Give me your poor, your tired, your huddled masses.' She's got a baseball bat and yelling, 'You want a piece of me?' (Robin Williams)

The shepherd drives the wolf from the sheep's throat, for which the sheep thanks the shepherd as his liberator, while the wolf denounces him for the same act as the destroyer of liberty. (Abraham Lincoln)

The rule is perfect: in all matters of opinion our adversaries are insane. (Mark Twain)

Jonathan Swift, in *The Art of Political Lying*, (1715): "There is one essential point wherein a political liar differs from others of the faculty, that he ought to have but a short memory, which is necessary, according to the various occasions he meets with every hour, of differing from himself, and swearing to both sides of a contradiction, as he finds the persons disposed with whom he hath to deal. The superiority of his genius consists in nothing else but an inexhaustible fund of political lies, which he plentifully distributes every minute he speaks, and by an unparalleled generosity forgets, and consequently contradicts, the next half hour. He never yet considered whether any proposition were true or false, but whether it were convenient for the present minute or company to affirm or deny it. I think he cannot with any justice be taxed with perjury, when he invokes God and Christ, because he hath often fairly given public notice to the world that he believes in neither."

Power does not corrupt. Fear corrupts...perhaps the fear of a loss of power. (John Steinbeck)

Patriotism is the willingness to kill and be killed for trivial reasons. (Bertrand Russell)

When the rich make war it's the poor that die. (Jean-Paul Sartre)

I believe that Ronald Reagan will someday make this country what it once was...an arctic wilderness. (Steve Martin)

Mankind must put an end to war, or war will put an end to mankind. (John F. Kennedy)

If you like Trump, his presence in the White House is a daily extravaganza of sticking it to pompous elites and querulous reporters. If you hate Trump, you wake up every day with some fresh outrage to turn over in your head and text your friends about. Whichever way, it's exhilarating. (Bret Stevens, *Time* magazine)

The powerful do what they wish and the weak suffer what they must. (Thucydides, Athenian historian and general, 460-395 B.C., *History of the Peloponnesian War*)

Capitalism's golden rule: Whoever has the gold makes the rules. (Anuradha Mittal)

Two huge problems in the U.S. are deficiencies of the political system: the enormous power of concentrated wealth in determining the outcome of elections and then the policies afterwards, and the destruction of the labor movement. (Noam Chomsky)

There's nothing revolutionary about violence. (Dave Cross)

Man's capacity for justice makes democracy possible, but man's inclination to injustice makes democracy necessary. (Reinhold Niebuhr)

When profit motives and property rights are considered more important than people, the giant triplets of racism, materialism and militarism are incapable of being conquered. (Martin Luther King, Jr; anti-Vietnam War speech, 1967)

Hey, I have an idea. How about we arm all the teachers and coaches, and train them at least two hours a week to be safe with all those guns we give them, and pay them for their training time, and bill all that to the NRA! Oh yes, and how about if we get to sue the NRA if any of those teachers, by accident or design, harm any students with those guns! That sounds fair. (Beth Fitchet Wood)

An institution is the lengthened shadow of a man. (Ralph Waldo Emerson)

All wars are fought twice, the first time on the battlefield, the second time in memory. (Viet Thanh Nguyen, American novelist)

People say satire is dead. It's not dead; it's alive and living in the White House. (Robin Williams)

We must make our choice: We may have democracy in this country, or we may have wealth concentrated in the hands of a few, but we cannot have both. (Supreme Court Justice Louis Brandeis)

This land is your land and this land is my land, sure, but the world is run by those that never listen to music anyway. (Bob Dylan)

Characteristic leaders display "the state of intoxication which power is said to inspire, the state in which you believe you are indispensable and can therefore do anything, absolutely anything you feel like, anything at all." (Margaret Atwood, *The Handmaid's Tale*)

Great paradigm shifts do not occur due to government; they do not occur because of companies. They occur because visionary people come out and inspire people, inspire the masses. Governments are always last.
 (Charles Darwin)

No struggle can ever succeed without women participating side by side with men. (Muhammad Ali Jinnah, lawyer, politician, founder of Pakistan)

Rome did not create a great empire by counsel. Rome did it by killing all those who opposed them. (Mongolian proverb)

In the councils of government, we must guard against the acquisition of unwarranted influence, whether sought or unsought, by the military-industrial complex. The potential for the disastrous rise of misplaced power exists, and will persist. (Dwight Eisenhower)

Why did Marx write in all lower case?...He hated capitalism. (*AARP Magazine*)

The only variable that can explain the high rate of mass shootings in America is its astronomical number of guns. Americans make up about 4.4 percent of the global population but own 42 percent of the world's guns.

Man is a strange animal; he doesn't like to read the handwriting on the wall unless his back is up against it.
 (Adlai Stevenson)

If ever time should come, when vain and aspiring men shall possess the highest seats in government, our country will stand in need of its experienced patriots to prevent its ruin. (Samuel Adams)

In America the word *revolution* is used to sell Pantyhose. (Rita Mae Brown, *New York Times* bestselling author)

In times of extremes, extremists win. Their ideology becomes a religion, anyone who doesn't puppet their views is seen as an apostate, a heretic or a traitor, and moderates in the middle are annihilated. The aim of ideology is to eliminate ambiguity. (Margaret Atwood)

I watch the news channels incessantly. All the news stories are about the election. All the commercials are Viagra and Cialis. Election, erection, election, erection! Either way we're screwed. (Bette Midler)

The tyrant, who in order to hold his power, suppresses every superiority, does away with good men, forbids education and light, controls every movement of the citizens and, keeping them under a perpetual servitude, wants them to grow accustomed to baseness and cowardice, has his spies everywhere to listen to what is said in the meetings, and spreads dissension and calumny among the citizens and impoverishes them, is obliged to make war in order to keep his subjects occupied and impose on them permanent need of a chief. (Aristotle, 384-322 B.C.)

Democracy is like a tambourine...not everyone can be trusted with it. (John Oliver)

I am also very proud to be a liberal. Why is that so terrible these days? The liberals were liberators: they fought slavery, fought for women to have the right to vote, fought against Hitler, Stalin, fought to end segregation, fought to end apartheid. Liberals put an end

153

to child labor and they gave us the five day work week. What's to be ashamed of? (Barbra Streisand)

I think it would be so much fun to be in the White House. (Kim Kardashian)

Democracy and capitalism have very different beliefs about the proper distribution of power. One [democracy] believes in a completely equal distribution of political power, 'one man, one vote,' while the other [capitalism] believes that it is the duty of the economically fit to drive the unfit out of business and into extinction. To put it in its starkest form, capitalism is perfectly compatible with slavery. Democracy is not. (Lester Thurow)

The whole problem with the world is that fools and fanatics are always so certain of themselves, but wiser people are so full of doubts. (Bertrand Russell)

Facts do not cease to exist because they are ignored. (Aldous Huxley)

A Gallup Pollster was taking a door-to-door survey: "Ma'am, what do you think is the biggest problem in this country; ignorance or apathy?" She replies, "I don't know and I don't care!"

Freedom isn't free. It shouldn't be a bragging point that 'Oh, I don't get involved with politics,' as if that makes someone cleaner. No, that makes you derelict of duty in a republic. Liars and panderers in government would have a much harder time of it if so many people didn't insist on their right to remain ignorant and blindly agreeable. (Bill Maher)

One way to make sure crime doesn't pay would be to let the government run it. (Ronald Reagan)

During the Vietnam War, which lasted longer than any war we've ever been in, and which we lost, every respectable artist in this country was against the war. It was like a laser beam. We were all aimed in the same direction. The power of this weapon turns out to be that of a custard pie dropped from a stepladder six feet high. (Kurt Vonnegut)

Laughter has no foreign accent. (Paul Lowney, 1917-2007, Seattle-based author and humorist)

All the problems we face in the United States today can be traced back to an unenlightened immigration policy on the part of the American Indian. (Pat Paulsen)

Middle class jobs prevent crime and violence. (Michael Moore)

The most common way people give up their power is by thinking they don't have any. (Alice Walker)

The fate of our country is now in the hands of people who don't think about what they want until they get right up to the register at McDonald's. (Steven Colbert)

A nation that forgets its past has no future. (Winston Churchill)

When Ronald Reagan was elected I was on a bus traveling with a band in France. I wrote a little arrangement of The Star Spangled Banner in a minor key. (Carla Bley)

Today, whether it is a student who holds a sit-in to get the army recruiters off his campus, or the mother of a dead soldier who refuses to leave the front gate of the president's ranch, we continue to be saved by brave people who risk ridicule and rejection but end up turning huge tides of public opinion in the direction of righteousness. We owe them enormous debts of gratitude. It is not easy to stand up for what is right, especially when everybody else is afraid to leave the comfortable path of conformity. (Michael Moore)

There are men in government who shouldn't be allowed to play with matches. (Will Rogers)

I should like to love my country and still love justice. (Albert Camus)

I cannot believe that war is the best solution. No one won the last war, and no one will win the next war. (Eleanor Roosevelt)

Before there were unions, there was no middle class. (Michael Moore)

It is amazing what you can accomplish if you do not care who gets the credit. (Harry S. Truman)

You can always count on Americans to do the right thing, after they've tried everything else. (Winston Churchill)

A citizen of America will cross the ocean to fight for democracy but won't cross the street to vote in a national election. (Bill Vaughn)

This republic was not established by cowards, and cowards will not preserve it. (Elmer Davis,1890-1958, news reporter, author, Director of the United States Office of War Information during World War II,)

Four big hits and seven licks ago, our before-daddies swung forth upon this sweet groovy land a swingin', stompin'. jumpin', blowin', wailin' new nation, hip to the

156

cool groove of liberty, and solid-sent with the ace lick that all studs, chicks, cats and kitties, red white or blue, are created level in front. (Lord Buckley)

All politicians should have 3 hats: one to throw into the ring, one to talk through, and one to pull rabbits out of if elected. (Carl Sandburg)

One can resist the invasion of armies; one cannot resist the invasion of ideas. (Victor Hugo)

Freedom is not worth fighting for if it means no more than license for everyone to get as much as he can for himself. (Dorothy Canfield Fisher)

I would like to electrocute everyone who uses the word 'fair' in connection with income tax policies. (William F. Buckley, Jr.)

If voting made any difference they wouldn't let us do it. (Mark Twain)

I don't want anything seventy-thirty. Fifty-fifty's always good enough for me. I don't want to have to give anybody seventy; I don't want anybody to give me seventy. I want fifty. (James Dean)

When the President does it, that means that it is not illegal. (Richard Nixon)

America is the wealthiest nation on Earth, but its people are mainly poor, and poor Americans are urged to hate themselves…it is in fact a crime for an American to be poor, even though America is a nation of poor. Every other nation has folk traditions of men who were poor but extremely wise and virtuous, and therefore more estimable than anyone with power or gold. No such tales are told by American poor. They mock themselves and glorify their betters. (Kurt Vonnegut)

I'm not against the police; I'm just afraid of them. (Alfred Hitchcock)

Politicians and diapers must be changed often and for the same reason. (Mark Twain)

I have left orders to be awakened at any time during national emergency, even if I'm in a cabinet meeting. (Ronald Reagan)

If you don't have a seat at the table, you're probably on the menu. (Elizabeth Warren)

If 40 million people say a foolish thing it does not become a wise one. (W. Somerset Maugham)

If you can't make them see the light, make them feel the heat. (David Gergen, Harvard Professor, presidential advisor, former editor of *U.S. News and World Report*)

The best way to stop a bad guy with a gun is 75.4 million Millennials with a vote. (Jenna Blum, American novelist)

What nation's capital is growing the fastest?...Ireland. It's Dublin every year.

Elections belong to the people. It's their decision. If they decide to turn their backs on the fire and burn their behinds, then they will just have to sit on their blisters. (Abraham Lincoln)

In politics, stupidity is not a handicap. (Napoleon Bonaparte)

We'll see what happens. (Donald J. Trump)

This war isn't about terrorism; it's about oil. If the principal export of Iraq were palm dates, we wouldn't be there. (Stan Goff, American anti-war activist, writer, blogger)

One fifth of the people are against everything all the time. (Robert Kennedy)

We dare not forget today that we are the heirs of that first revolution. (John F. Kennedy)

I think Kennedy being assassinated changed the world. That shot changed everything about America, and made us cynical, made people discontented and angry. (Robert Osbourne, 1932–2017, American actor, film historian, author)

If Rosa Parks had taken a poll before she sat down in the bus in Montgomery, she'd still be standing. (Mary Francis Berry, American Historian, UNIV Penn)

Against logic there is no armor like ignorance.

Ours is a government of checks and balances. The Mafia and crooked businessmen make out checks, and the politicians and other compromised officials improve their bank balances. (Steve Allen)

There is a tragic flaw in our precious Constitution, and I don't know what can be done to fix it. This is it: Only nut cases want to be president. (Kurt Vonnegut)

I find it ironic that the colors red, white, and blue stand for freedom, until they're flashing behind you. (Tom Newbill)

The thing the sixties did was to show us the possibilities and the responsibility that we all had. It wasn't the answer. It just gave us a glimpse of the possibility. (John Lennon)

Democracy is not a spectator sport. (Bernie Sanders)

In nuclear war all men are cremated equal. (Dexter Gordon)

Some men change their party for the sake of their principles; others change their principles for the sake of their party. (Winston Churchill)

In war there are no winners, only widows. (Eric Heisserer, *Arrival*)

Times have not become more violent. They've just become more televised. (Marilyn Manson)

The presidency doesn't change who you are, the presidency reveals who you are. (Michelle Obama)

RESPECT EXISTENCE OR EXPECT RESISTANCE. (Slogan on sign)

I looked up the word "politics" in the dictionary, and it's actually a combination of two words: "poli," which means "many," and "tics," which means "bloodsuckers." (Jay Leno)

1BY2SEA (License Plate)

I am opposing a social order in which it is possible for one man who does absolutely nothing that is useful, to amass a fortune of hundreds of millions of dollars, while millions of men and women who work all the days of their lives secure barely enough for a wretched existence. (Eugene V. Debs)

The enemy isn't conservatism. The enemy isn't
liberalism. The enemy is bullshit. (Lars Erik Nelson)

Trapped by Sparrow:
Trump
blundered
into the
White
House,
and now
he's
trapped,
like a
moose
in a
shopping mall.

What's the difference between Death and
Taxes?...Congress doesn't meet every year to make
Death worse.

We need a president who is fluent in at least one
language. (Buck Henry)

But even the President of the United States must
sometimes have to stand naked. (Bob Dylan, *It's Alright
Ma, I'm Only Bleeding*, 1965)

If you ever see me getting beaten by the police, put
down the video camera and come help me. (Bobcat
Goldthwait)

In my lifetime, we've gone from Eisenhower to George
W. Bush. We've gone from John F. Kennedy to Al Gore.
If this is evolution, I believe that in twelve years, we'll be
voting for plants. (Lewis Black)

In a country well governed, poverty is something to be ashamed of. In a country badly governed, wealth is something to be ashamed of. (Confucius)

When I was a boy I was told that anybody could become president. I'm beginning to believe it. (Clarence Darrow)

There are advantages to being elected president. The day after I was elected, I had my high school grades classified Top Secret. (Ronald Reagan)

If we could just find out who's in charge, we could kill him. (George Carlin)

The buck stops here. (Harry S. Truman)

One law for the lion and the ox is oppression. (William Blake)

A people unaware of its myths is likely to continue living by them, though the world around that people may change and demand changes in their psychology, their ethics and their institutions. (Richard Slotkin, Professor, Wesleyan University)

Those who rightly challenge the assumptions of others become slowly more indignant at any challenge to their own. (Wilkinson, *All Falling Faiths*)

The best defense against bullshit is vigilance. So if you smell something, say something. (Jon Stewart)

Now, don't get me wrong, I think border security is important. And I have no doubt that the Republican plan will put a stop to the number one threat facing America today: illegal cleaning ladies. (Bill Maher)

Status Quo, you know, is Latin for 'the mess we're in'. (Ronald Reagan)

America is really where the experiment is unfolding. This is really where the races confront one another, where the classes, where the genders, where even the sexual orientations confront one another. This is the real laboratory of democracy. (Leonard Cohen)

Compassion is the radicalism of our time. (The Dalai Lama)

If we say, "The government sucks," we're kinda saying that we suck. (Michael Moore)

You have to remember one thing about the will of the people: It wasn't that long ago that we were swept away by the Macarena. (Jon Stewart)

If the facts are against you, argue the law. If the law is against you, argue the facts. If the law and the facts are against you, pound the table and yell like hell. (Carl Sandburg)

I am proud to offer my endorsement of Donald J. Trump for President of the United States. He is a successful executive and entrepreneur, a wonderful father, and a man who I believe can lead our country to greatness again. (Jerry Falwell Jr., President of the Liberty University)

I realized that this was the big secret of democracy--that change can occur by starting off with just a few people doing something. (Michael Moore)

RACE

How are we going to get rid of racism? Stop talking
about it! (Morgan Freeman)

The animals of the world exist for their own reasons.
They were not made for humans any more than black
people were made for white, or women created for
men. (Alice Walker)

The legal battle against segregation is won, but the
community battle goes on. (Dorothy Day)

Obama was the best thing for black nerds everywhere.
Finally we had a role model. Before Obama, we basically
had Urkel. (Jordan Peele, American filmmaker, actor)

He's not America's first black president. He's America's
first mixed-race president. (Morgan Freeman)

Mozart, Pascal, Boolean algebra, Shakespeare,
parliamentary government, baroque churches, Newton,
the emancipation of women, Kant, Balanchine ballets, et
al. don't redeem what this particular civilization has
wrought upon the world. The white race is the cancer of
human history. (Susan Sontag)

Hockey is a sport for white men. Basketball is a sport for
black men. Golf is a sport for white men dressed like
black pimps. (Tiger Woods)

Music played a large role in the survival of black people
in America--that and a sense of humor that just couldn't
be enslaved. (Redd Foxx)

When I was nine years old, *Star Trek* came on. I looked
at it and went screaming through the house, 'Come here,
mum, everybody, come quick, come quick, there's a

black lady on television and she ain't no maid!' I knew right then and there I could be anything I wanted to be. (Whoopi Goldberg)

I think all in all, one thing a lot of plays seem to be saying is that we need to, as black Americans, to make a connection with our past in order to determine the kind of future we're going to have. In other words, we simply need to know who we are in relation to our historical presence in America. (August Wilson, 1945-2005, American playwright)

When I was a kid, some of the guys would try to get me to hate white people for what they've been doing to Negroes, and for a while I tried real hard. But every time I got to hating them, some white guy would come along and mess the whole thing up. (Thelonious Monk)

The simple truth is that balding African-American men look cool when they shave their heads, whereas balding white men look like giant thumbs. (Dave Barry, American author and columnist)

People live in their part of the Union, and if they don't travel a lot, then there is a tendency to believe that the other parts of America couldn't possibly be as American as their part. You can see it in the way people in the South scrunch up their faces when they hear words like 'New York,' 'Chicago,' and 'challah.' (W. Kamau Bell)

A lot of shelter dogs are mutts like me. (Barack Obama)

I don't see much future for the Americans...it's a decayed country. And they have their racial problem, and the problem of social inequalities...my feelings against Americanism are feelings of hatred and deep repugnance...everything about the behaviour of American society reveals that it's half Judaized, and the other half negrified. How can one expect a State like that to hold together? (Adolf Hitler)

Segregation shaped me; education liberated me. (Maya Angelou)

Dr. Martin Luther King is not a black hero. He is an American hero. (Morgan Freeman)

Don't terrorize, organize. Don't burn, give kids a chance to learn. The real answer to race problems in this country is education. Not burning and killing. Be ready. Be qualified. Own something. Be somebody. That's black power. (James Brown)

I went to Europe at 19, and it turned me upside down in many ways. It gave you some sense of perspective of past, present and future. It took the myopic conflict between just black and white in the United States and put it on another level because you saw the turmoil between the Armenians and the Turks, and the Cypriots and the Greeks, and the Swedes and the Danes, and the Koreans and the Japanese. Everybody had these hassles, and you saw it was a basic part of human nature, these conflicts. It opened my soul, it opened my mind. (Quincy Jones)

I am just mystified by these people telling me I would think Obama was doing a great job if his skin contained less melanin. (Jonah Goldberg)

I found this out over the years, that racism is a thinly veiled disguise over economics and money. It really is. (Quincy Jones)

I think it's helpful to remind white ethnics that they, too, came here in boats. (Tom Hayden)

We must come to the point where we realize the concept of race is a false one. There is only one race, the human race. (Dan Aykroyd)

During my lifetime I have dedicated myself to this struggle of the African people. I have fought against white domination, and I have fought against black domination. I have cherished the ideal of a democratic and free society in which all persons live together in harmony and with equal opportunities. It is an ideal which I hope to live for and to achieve. But if needs be, it is an ideal for which I am prepared to die. (Nelson Mandela)

The white man's happiness cannot be purchased by the black man's misery. (Frederick Douglass)

Every town has the same two malls: the one white people go to and the one white people used to go to. (Chris Rock)

What was beautiful about slavery? Nothing, rationally! But the spirituals, folklore, slave religion, and slave narratives are beautiful, and they came out of slavery. How do we explain that miracle? What's beautiful about lynching and Jim Crow segregation? Nothing! Yet the blues, jazz, great preaching, and gospel music are beautiful, and they came out of the post-slavery brutalities of white supremacy. In the 1960s we proclaimed 'Black is beautiful!' because it is. We raised our fists to 'I'm Black and I'm Proud,' and we showed 'Black Pride' in our walk and talk, our song and sermon. (James H. Cone)

My name is Arsenio. That's a very unique name for a black man. In Greek it means Leroy. (Arsenio Hall)

(January, 1861)
Confederate States of America--Mississippi Secession

"A Declaration of the Immediate Causes Which Induce and Justify the Secession of the State of Mississippi from the Federal Union.

In the momentous step which our State has taken of dissolving its connection with the government of which we so long formed a part, it is but just that we should declare the prominent reasons which have induced our course.

Our position is thoroughly identified with the institution of slavery--the greatest material interest of the world. Its labor supplies the product which constitutes by far the largest and most important portions of commerce of the earth. These products are peculiar to the climate verging on the tropical regions, and by an imperious law of nature, none but the black race can bear exposure to the tropical sun. These products have become necessities of the world, and a blow at slavery is a blow at commerce and civilization. That blow has been long aimed at the institution, and was at the point of reaching its consummation. There was no choice left us but submission to the mandates of abolition, or a dissolution of the Union, whose principles had been subverted to work out our ruin."

Hip-hop has done so much for racial relations, and I don't think it's given the proper credit. It has changed America immensely. I'm gonna make a very bold statement: Hip-hop has done more than any leader, politician, or *anyone* to improve race relations. (Jay-Z)

You didn't know if Chuck Berry was black or white. It was not a concern. (Keith Richards)

I'm most biased about how white people have to learn to shut up when the conversation of racism comes up. White people have to learn to listen. Whether they agree with what they're hearing or not, they have to know to shut up and listen. (W. Kamau Bell)

I love being famous. It's almost like being white. (Chris Rock)

I think that wealthy white people would like to have a country that resembles the Fifties, when all the minorities were tucked away in ghettos and paid in very low wages but on the surface it was very bright and shiny and free and the rest of the world would look on it longingly. (Alice Walker)

We had the best organization the black man had ever seen. Niggers ruined it. (Spike Lee, *Malcom X,* 1992)

To some extent Doctor King's been a buffer between the black community and the white community. White people don't know it, but the white people's best friend is dead. (Jesse Jackson, shortly after King's assassination)

People, I just want to say, can we all get along? Can we all get along? (Rodney King)

169

RIDDLES

1) What has no beginning, end, or middle?

2) I have two coins that up to 30 cents. One is not a nickel. What are the two coins?

3) A man leaves home and turns left three times, only to return home facing two men that are wearing masks. Who are these two men?

4) You're running a race and pass the person in 2nd place. What place are you now?

5) What can travel around the world while staying in a corner?

6) Johnny's mother had three children. The first was named April and the second was named May. What was the name of the third child?

7) If there are three apples and you take two away, how many apples do you have?

8) The more it dries, the wetter it gets. What is it?

9) What goes up and down but never moves?

10) What has one head, one foot, and four legs?

   1- A doughnut.
   2- A quarter and a nickel.
   3- A catcher and umpire.
   4- 2nd place.
   5- A stamp.
   6- Johnny.
   7- You took two apples, so now you have two of them.

8- A towel.
9- The temperature.
10- A bed.

When George W. Bush was elected President of the
United States, early on he had a meeting with the Queen
of England.
President: Your Majesty. Do you have any tips on
how to be a good leader?
Queen: Well, you should surround yourself with
intelligent people.
President: How do you know if they're intelligent?
Queen: You could ask them a riddle. Let me illustrate.
(To her staff) Please bring me Tony Blair (Prime
Minister)...Tony, please answer this riddle: Your parents
have a child. It's not your brother. It's not your sister.
Who is it?
Tony: That would be me.
Queen: Very good. Thanks, Tony.
President: Hmmm.
The President flies back to Washington thinking of this.
He calls Dick Cheney (Vice President) into the oval
office.
President: Dick. Answer this riddle: Your parents
have a kid. It's not your brother. It's not your sister. Who
is it?
VP: (Scratching his head) I'll have to get back to you
on that one.
The VP leaves the office and scrambles around the
West Wing until he runs into Colin Powell (Secretary of
State).
VP: Colin, you're a smart guy. Answer this question.
Your parents have a kid. It's not your brother. It's not
your sister. Who is it?
Colin; Well, that would be me.
VP: Thanks, Colin.
The VP runs back to the oval office and announces to
the President:

VP: Mr. President...it's Colin Powell!
President: No, you idiot, It's Tony Blair!

RIMSHOT DANDIES

I picked up a hitchhiker last night. He seemed surprised that I'd pick up a stranger and asked "Thanks, but why would you pick me up? How do you know I'm not a serial killer" I told him the odds of two serial killers being in one car would be astronomical. (Tom Newbill)

Where does an 800 lb. gorilla sleep?...anywhere it wants.

What did the blonde say as she drove past a YMCA?..."Look! Someone misspelled MACY'S!"

A young ventriloquist is touring Norway and puts on a show in a small fishing town. With his dummy on his knee, he starts going through his usual dumb blonde jokes.

Suddenly, a blonde woman in the fourth row stands on her chair and starts shouting, "I've heard enough of your stupid blonde jokes. What makes you think you can stereotype Norwegian blonde women that way? What does the color of a woman's hair have to do with her worth as a human being? It's men like you who keep women like me from being respected at work and in the community, and from reaching our full potential as people. Its people like you that make others think that all blondes are dumb! You and your kind continue to perpetuate discrimination against not only blondes, but women in general, pathetically all in the name of humor!" The embarrassed ventriloquist begins to apologize, and the blonde interrupts yelling, "You stay out of this! I'm talking to that little shit on your lap." (Tom Newbill)

Two cannibals were eating a clown. One cannibal turned to the other and asked, "Does this taste funny to you?"

173

Why did the cannibal go to the smorgasbord?...It was only ten dollars a head.

Cannibal Husband: "I don't like your Mother."
Cannibal Wife: "Try the potatoes." (Johnny Ratz)

Do you know why it's so hard to solve a redneck murder?...There are no dental records and all the DNA is the same. (Jeff Foxworthy)

A husband and wife are riding along in their car. He is driving but does not have his safety belt fastened. A motorcycle cop sees this as he passes and spins a "U" to pull the car over. Meantime, the driver, seeing the cop, has fastened his seat belt. The cop steps up to the driver's window and says, "I'm gonna have to give you a ticket for driving with an unfastened safety belt."

The driver loudly argues, "Officer, as you can *plainly* see, I have my safety belt *on*. I *always* put my safety belt on *immediately* when I first get in the car." The cop sighs and looks into the car to the wife, who is sitting on the right. "Ma'am, you look like a reasonable person. Did he have his safety belt on when I first passed him?"

"Officer, I have to say 'yes.' After 20 years of marriage I've learned that you don't argue with my husband when he's been drinkin'."

Knock, knock
Who's there?
Eskimos, Christians, and Italians
Eskimos, Christians, and Italians who?
Eskimos, Christians, and Italians no lies (*)

(*) Ask me no questions and I'll tell you no lies.

I'm taking Viagra and drinking prune juice--I don't know if I'm coming or going. (Rodney Dangerfield)

I never think that people die. They just go to department stores. (Andy Warhol)

You can't have everything. Where would you put it? (Steven Wright)

What happens when you cross a policeman with a skunk?...Law and odor!

SCHOOL

I was a smart kid, but I hated school. (Eminem)

America believes in education: the average professor earns more money in a year than a professional athlete earns in a whole week. (Evan Esar, 1899-1995, American humorist)

If you ever have a kid that doesn't know what to do, stick him in art school. It's amazing what evolves. (Ridley Scott, English film director)

I swallowed a whole dictionary. Now I have thesaurus throat ever. (T-shirt)

Reading is equivalent to thinking with someone else's head instead of with one's own. (Arthur Schopenhauer)

I would at times feel that learning to read had been a curse rather than a blessing; it had given me a view of my wretched condition, without the remedy. (Frederick Douglass)

Academia: the secular priesthood. (Dave Cross)

Did you hear about the new anti-gravity book?...You can't put it down.

A library doesn't need windows. A library *is* a window. (Stewart Brand, American writer, editor of the *Whole Earth Catalog*)

There is no significant idea which cannot be explained to an intelligent twelve-year-old boy in fifteen minutes. (Leo Tolstoy)

I'm not a teacher, but an awakener. (Robert Frost)

176

Reason functions by integrating perceptual data into concepts. (Ayn Rand)

With all the classes they offer at school, how come they don't have one for common sense? (Gabriel Iglesias, American comedian, actor, writer)

If only I'd known my differentness would be an asset, then my earlier life would have been much easier. (Bette Midler)

I've never seen 'Seinfeld,' never seen 'The Cosby Show.' I just don't watch it. I saw half of 'Oprah' one time. I'd rather read. (August Wilson, 1945-2005, American playwright)

Three things are needed to educate the peasantry: schools, schools, and schools. (Leo Tolstoy)

I dropped out of school, but I didn't drop out of life. I would leave the house each morning and go to the main branch of the Carnegie Library in Oakland where they had all the books in the world. I felt suddenly liberated from the constraints of a pre-arranged curriculum that labored through one book in eight months. (August Wilson)

Keep your mouth closed, and let your eyes listen. (Lil Wayne)

Books are a time machine. (Jonathan Nolan, English-American screenwriter, television producer)

The America I loved still exists, if not in the White House or the Supreme Court or the Senate or the House of Representatives or the media. The America I love still exists at the front desks of our public libraries. (Kurt Vonnegut)

We are all geniuses up to the age of ten. (Aldous Huxley)

Knowing you have something good to read before bed is among the most pleasurable of sensations. (Vladimir Nabokov)

If you think in terms of a year, plant a seed; if in terms of ten years, plant trees; if in terms of 100 years, teach the people. (Confucius)

If I were again beginning my studies, I would follow the advice of Plato and start with mathematics. (Galileo Galilei)

I disagree with people who think you learn more from getting beat up than you do from winning, (Tom Cruise)

You cannot get an A if you're afraid of getting an F. (Quincy Jones)

Only someone who is well prepared has the opportunity to improvise. (Ingmar Bergman)

The soul without imagination is what an observatory would be without a telescope. (Henry Ward Beecher)

Spend time with people who know how to use their days well. Just as iron sharpens iron, positive people will inspire you to be positive. (Rihanna)

Teenagers these days are out of control. They eat like pigs, they are disrespectful of adults, they interrupt and contradict their parents, and they terrorize their teachers. (Aristotle 384-322 B.C.)

I spent three days a week for 10 years educating myself in the public library, and it's better than college. People should educate themselves. You can get a complete education for no money. At the end of 10 years, I had read every book in the library and had written a thousand stories. (Ray Bradbury)

The Past, The Present and The Future all walk into a bar...It was tense. (T-shirt)

No schooling is needed to become a fool. (Mexican proverb)

I first had the idea of writing a popular book about the universe in 1982. My intention was partly to earn money to pay my daughter's school fees. (Stephen Hawking)

If skill could be gained by watching, every dog would become a butcher. (Turkish proverb)

When I was a teenager, I began to settle into school because I'd discovered the extracurricular activities that interested me, music and theater. (Morgan Freeman)

It's amazing how much you can learn if your intentions are truly earnest. (Chuck Berry)

In schools students gather information, but not always insight. (Arthur Schopenhauer)

I actually think the reason I am interested in certain parts is because I was such a dweeb in high school. When you are such a loser, it's a helpful way in to a lot of characters because even very powerful people are not all that powerful, really. (Sigourney Weaver)

Literacy could be the ladder out of poverty. (Morgan Freeman)

There is no education like adversity. (Benjamin Disraeli)

Knowledge gives your imagination more to work with. (Will Brady)

I was never top of the class at school, but my classmates must have seen potential in me, because my nickname was 'Einstein.' (Stephen Hawking)

I was not a good student. I did not spend much time at college; I was too busy enjoying myself. (Stephen Hawking)

When I was in junior high school, the teachers voted me the student most likely to end up in the electric chair. (Sylvester Stallone)

When I was in high school, I earned the pimple award and every other gross-out award. (Jack Nicholson)

I'd be satisfied just coaching in high school. I turned down a number of colleges when I was teaching in South Bend, Indiana, before I went into the service. I honestly believe that if I hadn't enlisted in the service, I would never have left high school teaching. I'm sure I would have never left. (John Wooden, 1910-2010, basketball player and head coach UCLA)

Arts education is a big part of building a 21st century creative mind, and I think we have let way too many kids lose their way by not drawing in their young minds with music, dance, painting and other various ways we can express those things we do not have words for. (Heather Watts)

What sculpture is to a block of marble, education is to the soul. (Joseph Addison, 1672-1719, English essayist, poet, playwright, and politician)

To teach is to learn twice. (Joseph Joubert)

Teacher: I don't think you're cut out to be a mime.
Student: Was it something I said?
Teacher: Yes. (*AARP Magazine*)

To travel far, there is no better ship than a book (Emily Dickenson)

What's the longest punctuation mark?...The hundred-yard dash.

I never made a mistake in grammar but one in my life and as soon as I done it I seen it. (Carl Sandburg)

Listen, here's the thing about an English degree--if you sat somebody down and asked them to make a list of the writers they admire over the last hundred years, see how many of them got a degree in English. (David Mamet)

I have always imagined that Paradise will be a kind of library. (Jorge Luis Borges)

I won't say ours was a tough school, but we had our own coroner. We used to write essays like: "What I'm going to be if I grow up." (Lenny Bruce)

I think the big mistake in schools is trying to teach children using fear as the basic motivation. Fear of getting failing grades, fear of not staying up with your class, etc. Interest can produce learning on a scale compared to fear as a nuclear explosion to a firecracker. (Stanley Kubrick)

I quit college so fast I didn't even clean out my locker. (Steven Spielberg)

Change is the end result of all true learning. (Leo Buscaglia, 1924-1998, American author)

A good teacher who can take the zero pay and help kids develop physically, emotionally, socially, is literally an angel. (Eva Amurri, American film and television actress)

SCIENCE & TECHNOLOGY

Equipped with his five senses, man explores the universe around him and calls the adventure Science. (Edwin Hubble)

YOU MATTER. Unless you multiply yourself by the speed of light...then YOU ENERGY. (T-shirt)

We don't know a millionth of one percent about anything. (Thomas A. Edison)

My goal is simple. It is complete understanding of the universe, why it is as it is and why it exists at all. (Stephan Hawking)

There is just one thing I can promise you about the outer-space program...your tax dollar will go a lot further. (Wernher von Braun)

The universe has been made neither by gods nor men, but it has been, and is, and will be eternally. (Heraclitus, circa 545-475 B.C., Greek philosopher)

Technological progress has merely provided us with more efficient means for going backwards. (Aldous Huxley)

All truths are easy to understand once they are discovered; the point is to discover them. (Galileo Galilei)

Logic will get you from A to B. Imagination will take you everywhere. (Albert Einstein)

Television has proved that people will look at anything rather than each other. (Ann Landers)

183

The cloning of humans is on most of the list of things to worry about from Science, along with behavior control, genetic engineering, transplanted heads, computer poetry and the unrestrained growth of plastic flowers.
   (Lewis Thomas, 1913-1993, American Physician)

The only real number is one, the rest are mere repetition. (Vladimir Nabokov)

No man ever steps in the same river twice, for it's not the same river and he's not the same man. (Heraclitus)

'Faith' is a fine invention, when gentlemen can see, But microscopes are prudent in an emergency.
   (Emily Dickinson)

When scientific power outruns moral power, we end up with guided missiles and misguided men. (Martin Luther King, Jr.)

Islands are natural workshops of evolution. (Richard Dawkins)

If I have seen further it is by standing on the shoulders of giants. (Sir Isaac Newton)

Heisenberg, Max Plank and Einstein, they all agreed that science could not solve the mystery of the universe.
   (Harry Dean Stanton, American actor)

What is now proved was once only imagined. (William Blake)

My dad took me out to see a meteor shower when I was a little kid, and it was scary for me because he woke me up in the middle of the night. My heart was beating, I didn't know what he wanted to do. He wouldn't tell me, and he put me in the car and we went off, and I saw all these people lying on blankets, looking up at the sky. (Steven Spielberg)

The days of the digital watch are numbered. (Tom Stoppard)

Computers are like Old Testament gods; lots of rules and no mercy. (Joseph Campbell)

Science is the captain, and practice the soldiers. (Leonardo da Vinci)

My eyes are constantly wide open to the extraordinary fact of existence. Not just human existence, but the existence of life and how this breathtakingly powerful process, which is natural selection, has managed to take the very simple facts of physics and chemistry and build them up to redwood trees and humans. (Richard Dawkins)

Television is the triumph of machine over people. (Fred Allen, American comedian, 1894-1956)

Science is organized knowledge. Wisdom is organized life. (Immanuel Kant)

I believe in intuitions and inspirations. I sometimes *feel* that I am right. I do not *know* that I am. (Albert Einstein)

Science is increasingly answering questions that used to be the province of religion. (Stephen Hawking)

Why can you never trust atoms?...They make up everything!

To say that a man is made up of certain chemical elements is a satisfactory description only for those who intend to use him as a fertilizer. (Hermann Joseph Miller, 1890-1967, geneticist, Nobel Prize, 1946)

Never trust a computer you can't throw out a window. (Steve Wozniak)

I'll always remember--when I was a kid, I shook hands with Orville Wright. Forty years later, I shook hands with Neal Armstrong. The guy that invented the airplane and the guy that walked on the moon. In a lifetime, that's kinda wild when you think about it. (Jonathan Winters)

Two truths cannot contradict one another. (Galileo Galilei)

Fire is our first form of technology. (Ridley Scott, English film director and producer)

Mathematics is not arithmetic. Though mathematics may have arisen from the practices of counting and measuring, it really deals with logical reasoning in which theorems--general and specific statements--can be deduced from the starting assumptions. It is, perhaps, the purist and the most rigorous of intellectual activities, and is often thought of as queen of the sciences. (Christopher Zeeman, 1925-2016, British mathematician)

The patent for toilet paper (1891) features an illustration that would imply the correct way the roll should be placed would be so the paper hangs over and not under.

Technology feeds on itself. Technology makes more technology possible. (Alvin Toffler)

Two things are infinite: the universe and human stupidity; and I'm not sure about the universe. (Albert Einstein)

If GM had kept up with technology like the computer industry has, we would all be driving $25 cars that got 1,000 MPG. (Bill Gates)

Getting information off the internet is like taking a drink from a fire hydrant. (Mitch Kapor, American computer software developer)

Technology is anything that wasn't around when you were born. (Alan Kay, American computer scientist)

Measure what can be measured, and make measurable what cannot be measured. (Galileo Galilei)

We have also arranged things so that almost no one understands science and technology. This is a prescription for disaster. We might get away with it for a while, but sooner or later this combustible mixture of ignorance and power Is going to blow up in our faces.
 (Carl Sagan)

Why did the physics teacher break up with the biology teacher?...No chemistry.

History is a vast early warning system. (Norman Cousins)

Research is what I'm doing when I don't know what I'm doing. (Wernher von Braun)

Science is magic that works. (Kurt Vonnegut)

The saddest aspect of life right now is that science gathers knowledge faster than society gathers wisdom.
 (Isaac Asimov)

JENIUS (T-shirt)

SIDEWAYS SENTENCES

I shall be so brief that I have already finished. (Salvador Dali)

Some things you teach yourself to remember to forget. (William Gibson)

If you lived in your car you'd be home by now.

Today was tomorrow yesterday, so don't inhale. (Mel Blanc, 1937-1989, 'The Man of 1000 Voices,' *Looney Tunes)*

I won't insult your intelligence by suggesting that you really believe what you just said. (William F. Buckley, Jr.)

Ineptitude is something at which I excel at.

One and one are, on occasion, eleven.

A cage went in search of a bird. (Franz Kafka)

I'm tired of talking about myself. What do you think about me?

There is no exception to the rule that every rule has an exception. (James Thurber)

Real knowledge is to know the extent of one's ignorance. (Confucius)

What you have become is the price you paid to get what you used to want. (Mignon McLaughlin)

Sometimes what you want you don't get until you don't want it anymore. (Ruth Gordon)

(Jiminy Cricket, as Pinocchio's conscience): "Now, you see, the world is full of temptations. They're the wrong things that seem right at the time, but, even though the right things may seem wrong sometimes, sometimes the wrong things may be right at the wrong time, or vice versa. Ahem. Understood?" (*Pinocchio,* 1940)

Half the lies they tell about me aren't true. (Yogi Berra)

My fake plants died because I did not pretend to water them. (Mitch Hedberg)

Remember, today is the tomorrow you worried about yesterday. (Dale Carnegie)

'Eleven plus two' is an anagram for 'Twelve plus one.'

If you rip a hole in a net, there are actually fewer holes in it than there were before.

I know you believe you understand what you think I said, but I'm not sure you realize that what you heard is not what I meant. (Robert McClosky)

SINGLE

There is no sovereignty like bachelorhood. (Turkish Proverb)

If I had a dollar for every girl that found me unattractive, they'd eventually find me attractive. (Tom Newbill)

A man can sleep around, no questions asked, but if a woman makes nineteen or twenty mistakes she's a tramp. (Joan Rivers)

Got ants in my pants and I need to dance, so big fine mama, come give me a chance. (James Brown)

I spent my whole single life trying to be thin just to find someone who'd love me once I got fat. (Stephanie Klein)

I was in love with a beautiful blonde once. She drove me to drink. That's the one thing I'm indebted to her for. (W. C. Fields)

'I am' is reportedly the shortest sentence in the English language. Could it be that 'I do' is the longest sentence? (George Carlin)

If I get dressed up, and my boyfriend says, 'You look gorgeous,' I kinda feel funny. I don't know if I'm particularly comfortable with being attractive. (Toni Collette)

A Cowboy Bath: more deodorant.

We have a saying in Germany: It is better to have loved and lost than to engage in a land war with Russia in the winter. (Heidi Klum)

Safe sex is great sex,
better wear latex,
'cause you don't want that late text,
that "I think I'm late" text.
  (Lil Wayne, *Lollipop* remix, 2008)

Some people can handle alcohol. You know who you
are. Some people can't handle alcohol. The police know
who you are. (Gabriel Iglesias)

I'm the last of the truly tacky women. I do trash with flash
and sleaze with ease. (Bette Midler)

Being divorced is like being hit by a Mack truck. If you
live through it, you start looking very carefully to the right
and to the left. (Jean Kerr)

I basically live out of my truck. I mean from place to
place. I feel more at home in my truck than just about
anywhere, which is a sad thing to say, but it's true. (Sam
Shepard)

Every woman deserves a man to ruin her lipstick, not her
mascara. (Charlotte Tilbury)

The worst thing about some men is that when they are
not drunk they are sober. (William Butler Yeats)

A tramp, a gentleman, a poet, a dreamer, a lonely fellow,
always hopeful of romance and adventure. (Charlie
Chaplin)

A man's only as old as the woman he feels. (Groucho
Marx)

Kiss me and you will see how important I am. (Sylvia
Plath)

I think genuine charm is an unmotivated interest in others. (Aretha Franklin)

Fred: I've been dating a girl who carries a Taser everywhere.
Ted: What's she like?
Fred: Stunning. (*AARP Magazine*)

A man's kiss is his signature. (Mae West)

A bachelor is a guy who never made the same mistake once. (Phyllis Diller)

Can we go back to using Facebook for what it was originally for...looking up exes to see how fat they got? (Bill Maher)

Make sure you marry someone who laughs at the same things you do. (J. D. Salinger)

You know you're in love when you can't fall asleep because reality is finally better than your dreams. (Dr. Seuss)

I've been on so many blind dates, I should get a free dog. (Wendy Liebman)

I think every girl's dream is to find a bad boy at the right time, when he wants to not be bad anymore. (Taylor Swift)

Men's magazines in the period immediately after World War II were almost all outdoor-oriented. They were connected to some extent in the male bonding that came out of a war... And what I tried to create was a magazine for the indoor guy, but focused specifically on the single life: in other words, the period of bachelorhood before you settle down. (Hugh Heffner, *Playboy* Magazine)

Being single is pretty good. It's a nice sense of irresponsibility. (Michael Douglas)

I don't drink these days. I am allergic to alcohol and narcotics. I break out in handcuffs. (Robert Downey, Jr.)

It's easy to fool the eye but it's hard to fool the heart. (Al Pacino)

I'm selfish, impatient and a little insecure. I make mistakes, I am out of control and at times hard to handle. But if you can't handle me at my worst, then you sure as hell don't deserve me at my best. (Marilyn Monroe)

Laugh and the world laughs with you. Snore and you sleep alone. (Anthony Burgess)

Plastic surgeons are always making mountains out of molehills. (Dolly Parton)

Nietzsche had a little one-liner on how to choose a wife. He said, "Are you willing to have a conversation with this woman for the next forty years?" (Kurt Vonnegut)

You're not drunk if you can lie on the floor without holding on. (Dean Martin)

Not to sound bad, but some girls are dumb. It's because they spend so much of their life trying to have the right look. On the other hand, some girls are just really smart. There are girls you can have conversations with that are really healthy conversations. You can argue real life issues and solve problems together. That is what makes a woman sexy. (Wale, American recording artist, record producer and actor)

I may not be much, but I'm all I ever think about.

193

A new cologne is coming out. It's for cowboys, and it's made from cow manure. That way the women will be on him like flies! (Bill Maher)

If I had to describe myself in one word, it would be 'needs improvement.'

A kiss can be a comma, a question mark, or an exclamation point. That's basic spelling that every woman ought to know. (Mistinguett, French actress and singer)

God is in my head, but the devil is in my pants. (Jonathan Winters)

Whenever I have to bid a hasty goodbye to a loved one, I've always made sure that my record collection was safely stored away in the boot of the car. (Robert Plant, lead singer in Led Zeppelin)

If a girl looks swell when she meets you, who gives a damn if she's late? Nobody. (J. D. Salinger)

I doubt if you can have a truly wild party without liquor. (Carl Sandburg)

Alimony is like buying hay for a dead horse. (Groucho Marx)

When I'm not in a relationship, I shave one leg. That way, when I sleep, it feels like I'm with a woman. (Gerry Shandling.)

You can't find true affection in Hollywood because everyone does the fake affection so well. (Carrie Fisher)

Sign outside: "NUDE BAR" Sign on door: "Sorry, we're clothed" (Steve Wood)

194

When are you going to realize that if doesn't apply to me, it doesn't matter? (Candice Bergen, TV sitcom *Murphy Brown*)

Personally, I think if a woman hasn't met the right man by the time she's 24, she may be lucky. (Deborah Kerr)

It is almost axiomatic that the best conversationalist is really the best listener. (Aretha Franklin)

I got so drunk last night that when I walked across the dance floor to get another drink, I won the dance contest. (Tom Newbill)

If you have someone that you think is The One, don't just sort of think in your ordinary mind, 'Okay. Let's pick a date. Let's plan this and make a party and get married.' Take that person and travel around the world. Buy a plane ticket for the two of you to travel all around the world, and go to places that are hard to go to and hard to get out of. And when you come back to JFK, when you land in JFK, and you're still in love with that person, get married at the airport. (Bill Murray)

SPIRIT

When the sun shines, it shines for everyone. (Ziggy Marley, seen in *Mutts*)

It's a sad and beautiful world. (Jim Jarmusch, filmmaker, *Down By Law*, 1986)

How do I define God? I don't. I see no need. (Noam Chomsky)

One of the conditions of enlightenment has always been a willingness to let go of what we thought we knew in order to appreciate truths we had never dreamed of. (Karen Armstrong, British author)

You believe in a book that has talking animals, wizards, witches, demons, sticks turning into snakes, burning bushes, food falling from the sky, people walking on water, and all sorts of magical, absurd and primitive stories, and you say that we are the ones that need help? (Mark Twain)

Learning how to be still, to really be still and let life happen...that stillness becomes a radiance. (Morgan Freeman)

I'm restless. Things are calling me away. My hair is being pulled by the stars again. (Anais Nin, 1903-1977, French-American writer)

Love is a fruit in season at all times, and within reach of every hand. (Mother Teresa)

Dear Jesus, do something. (Vladimir Nabokov)

Conceit is incompatible with understanding. (Leo Tolstoy)

Trust in Allah, but tie your camel. (Muslim proverb)

When an ordinary man attains knowledge, he is a sage; when a sage attains knowledge, he is an ordinary man. (Zen proverb)

Be submissive to everything, open, listening. (Jack Kerouac, *On the Road*, 1957)

It is a short walk from the hallelujah to the hoot. (Vladimir Nabokov)

The two most powerful warriors are patience and time. (Leo Tolstoy)

Each of us has his own alphabet with which to create poetry. (Irvine Stone)

I celebrate everyone's religious holidays. If it's good enough for the righteous, it's good enough for the self-righteous, I always say. (Bette Midler)

Until he extends his circle of compassion to include all living things, man will not himself find peace. (Albert Schweitzer)

The great tragedy of atheists is that they walk through this world and have no one to thank. (Leo Tolstoy)

Faith is not the belief that God will do what you want. It is the belief that God will do what is right. (Max Lucado, Christian preacher)

You don't have to see the whole staircase, just take the first step. (Martin Luther King, Jr.)

Mythology is what we call someone else's religion. (Joseph Campbell)

Atheism is a non-prophet organization. (George Carlin)

I don't believe in God because I don't believe in Mother Goose. (Clarence Darrow)

Where knowledge ends, religion begins. (Benjamin Disraeli)

My faith helps me understand that circumstances don't dictate my happiness, my inner peace. (Denzel Washington)

Love is an act of faith. (Erich Fromm)

A man from town approached the prophet and asked, "Prophet, please speak to us of Fate." The prophet closed his eyes in meditation, then looked toward Heaven and spoke: "It cuts through the sky on the wings of silver birds. It crosses the sea on the backs of giant ships. It zig-zags across the land on wheels of fire!"... After a pause, the man speaks, "But Prophet, that doesn't sound at all like fate." The prophet looks startled and says, "Oh, *Fate*! I thought you said *Freight!*"
  (Jackson Browne)

Every day you are happy is a gift to the rest of the world.
  (Harry Palmer, American actor)

Human psychology has the ability not to see things it doesn't want to see. (Chris Darwin)

Faith is universal. Our specific methods for understanding it are arbitrary. Some of us pray to Jesus, some of us go to Mecca, some of us study subatomic particles. In the end we are all just searching for truth, that which is greater than ourselves. (Dan Brown, American author)

Faith is much better than belief. Belief is when someone else does the thinking. (R. Buckminster Fuller)

Faith and doubt both are needed; not as antagonists, but working side by side to take us around the unknown curve. (Lillian Smith, 1897-1966, writer and social critic)

Faith is not contrary to reason. (Sherwood Eddy, 1871-1963, American Protestant missionary)

I don't fly on account of my religion. I'm a devout coward. (Henny Youngman)

I know what I'm giving up for Lent: my New Year's resolutions. (Henny Youngman)

You see, it's been our misfortune to have the wrong religion. Why didn't we have the religion of the Japanese, who regard sacrifice for the Fatherland as the highest good? The Mohammedan religion [Islam] too would have been more compatible to us than Christianity. Why did it have to be Christianity with its meekness and flabbiness? (Adolf Hitler)

Moses has revealed the existence of God to his nation, Jesus Christ to the Roman world, Muhammad to the old continent. (Napoleon Bonaparte)

Islam was like a mental cage. At first, when you open the door, the caged bird stays inside: it is frightened. It has internalized its imprisonment. It takes time for bird to escape, even after someone has opened the doors to its cage. (Ayaan Hirsi Ali)

All thinking men are atheists. (Ernest Hemingway)

A fanatic is one who can't change his mind and won't change the subject (Winston Churchill)

For God so loved the world, that he gave his only begotten Son, that whosoever believeth in him will believeth in anything. (Christopher Hitchens)

Morality is doing what is right, no matter what you are told. Religion is doing what you are told, no matter what is right. (H. L. Mencken)

Even the gods love jokes. (Plato)

My religious position: I think that God could do a lot better, and I'm willing to give Him the chance. (Mignon McLaughlin)

What if the meek inherited the Earth and we had to defend ourselves from Martians? (Robert Orben)

Religion is like a pair of shoes. Find one that fits for you, but don't make me wear your shoes. (George Carlin)

I think good things come to good people. (Derrick Rose, point guard Minnesota Timberwolves)

Faith consists in believing when it is beyond the power of reason to believe. (Voltaire)

Religion is all bunk. (Thomas Edison)

The way to see by faith is to shut the eye of reason.

Religion is nothing but the shadow cast by the universe on human intelligence. (Victor Hugo)

Question with boldness even the existence of a god. (Thomas Jefferson)

All the world is made of faith, and trust, and pixie dust. (J.M. Barrie, *Peter Pan*, 1906)

The beauty of religious mania is that logic can be happily tossed out the window. (Stephen King)

The whole idea of god is absurd. (Stanley Kubrick, American film director, screenwriter and producer, *2001: A Space Odyssey,* 1968)

There once was a time when all people believed in God and the church ruled. The time was called the Dark Ages. (Richard Lederer, American author, speaker, and teacher)

The church says the earth is flat, but I know that it is round, for I have seen the shadow on the moon, and I have more faith in a shadow than in the church.
 (Ferdinand Magellan, 1480-1521, Portuguese explorer)

Man is certainly stark mad; he cannot make a worm, yet he will make gods by the dozen. (Michel de Montaigne)

No free man needs a God. (Vladimir Nabokov)

Where there is evidence, no one speaks of 'faith'. We do not speak of faith that two and two are four or that the earth is round. (Bertrand Russell)

Faith is believing what you know ain't so. (Mark Twain)

Civilization will not attain its perfection until the last stone from the last church falls on the last priest. (Emile Zola)

I was happy enough to pray to any god, knowing that they were simply different faces created by men, of one individual truth. (Lian Hern)

Conscience is a man's compass. (Vincent van Gogh)

A nation that continues year after year to spend more on military defense than on programs of social uplift is approaching spiritual death. (Martin Luther King Jr.)

Giving advice to a stupid man is like giving salt to a squirrel. (Persian proverb)

I do not know what I may appear to the outside world, but to myself I seem to have been only like a boy playing on the seashore, and diverting himself in now and then finding a smoother pebble or a prettier shell than ordinary, whilst the great ocean of truth lay all undiscovered before me. (Isaac Newton)

God just has a way of working things out the way he wants to and you have no say in that. (Rihanna)

Abundance of knowledge does not teach men to be wise. (Heraclitus)

Between the Christianity of this land and the Christianity of Christ, I recognize the widest possible difference.
  (Frederick Douglass, 1818-1895, abolitionist, writer)

I would rather be the one who suffered wrong than the one who did wrong. The one who suffered wrong is stronger than the one who did wrong. Jesus was stronger than his crucifiers. Blacks are stronger than whites. Black religion is more creative and meaningful and true than white religion. That is why I love black religion, folklore, and the blues. Black culture keeps black people from hating white people. Every Sunday morning, we went to church to exorcize hate—of ourselves and of white racists. (James H. Cone, 1938-2018, theologian)

Help wanted. Inquire within. (Tom Newbill)

All trees are made of wood, but pine is not mahogany.
(Mexican proverb)

The governor of Texas, who, when asked if the *Bible*
should also be taught in Spanish, replied that "if English
was good enough for Jesus, then it's good enough for
me.' (Christopher Hitchens)

Religion is the masterpiece of the art of animal training,
for it trains people as to how they shall think. (Arthur
Schopenhauer)

When danger is in the past, God is forgotten. (Indian
proverb)

Love yourself first and everything else falls into line. You
really have to love yourself to get anything done in this
world. (Lucille Ball)

To the mind that is still, the whole universe surrenders.
(Lao Tzu)

A fallen blossom never returns to the branch. (Japanese
proverb)

Organized religion is primarily man putting words in
God's mouth. That's basically how I feel about that. But,
I do believe in believing and I admire it. I just don't think
it should be exclusive or judgmental. (Kathleen Turner)

Making itself intelligible is suicide for philosophy. (Martin
Heidegger)

Your sacred space is where you can find yourself again
and again. (Joseph Campbell)

Try to be a rainbow in someone's cloud. (Maya Angelou)

Some people who say to love your neighbor, in fact think it is right to hate people who do not do that. (Bertrand Russell)

If you don't scale the mountain, you can't view the plain. (Chinese proverb)

Tears come from the heart and not from the brain. (Leonardo da Vinci)

The greatest wisdom is to make the enjoyment of the present the supreme object of life; because that is the only reality, all else being merely the play of thought. (Arthur Schopenhauer)

Convictions are more dangerous foes of truth than lies. (Frederic Nietzsche)

For our sins God has created three enemies for us: mice in the house, the fox in the mountains, and a priest in our village. (South American proverb)

He who has no intelligence is happy with it. (South African proverb)

Knowing yourself is the beginning of all wisdom. (Aristotle)

The fishermen know that the sea is dangerous and the storm terrible, but they have never found these dangers sufficient reason for remaining ashore. (Vincent van Gogh)

Is he honest who resists his genius or conscience only for the sake of present ease or gratification? (William Blake)

Hope is a waking dream. (Aristotle)

The man being carried does not realize how far away the town really is. (Nigerian proverb)

One country, one ideology, one system is not sufficient. It is helpful to have a variety of different approaches. We can then make a joint effort to solve the problems of the whole of humankind. (Dalai Lama)

From the tree of silence we harvest the fruit of tranquility. (Peruvian proverb)

I would never want to be a member of a group whose symbol was a guy nailed to two pieces of wood. (George Carlin)

A blind man who sees is better than a sighted man who is blind. (Iranian proverb)

Gratitude is not only the greatest of virtues, but the parent of all the others. (Cicero)

Happiness is a quality of the soul, not a function of one's material circumstances. (Aristotle)

Thanks are the highest form of thought, and gratitude is happiness doubled by wonder. (G. K. Chesterton)

If the doors of perception were cleansed everything would appear to man as it is, Infinite. For man has closed himself up, till he sees all things thro' narrow chinks of his cavern. (William Blake)

A quiet and modest life brings more joy than a pursuit of success bound with constant unrest. (Albert Einstein)

What lies behind us and what lies ahead of us are tiny matters compared to what lives within us. (Henry David Thoreau)

Most people never have to face the fact that at the right time and the right place they're capable of anything. (Robert Towne, *Chinatown*)

The greatest deception men suffer is from their own opinions. (Leonardo da Vinci)

The first thing which I can record concerning myself is, that I was born. These are wonderful words. This life, to which neither time nor eternity can bring diminution--this everlasting living soul, began. My mind loses itself in these depths. (Groucho Marx)

Plow your field for a well-plowed field, not for possible harvests. (Zen proverb)

There are questions we could not get past if we were not set free from them by our very nature. (Franz Kafka)

Of all the things which wisdom provides to make us entirely happy, much the greatest is the possession of friendship. (Epicurus)

In life, all good things come hard, but wisdom is the hardest to come by. (Lucille Ball)

You will never do anything in this world without courage. It is the greatest quality of the mind next to honor. (Aristotle)

The power of mercy is that it belongs to the undeserving. (Bryan Stevenson, American lawyer, founder and executive director of the Equal Justice Initiative)

The glory of Christianity is to conquer by forgiveness. (William Blake)

The most difficult of all positions to attain: have nothing more to pray for. (Tacitus, *Germania*)

Religion is capable of driving people to such dangerous folly that faith seems to me to qualify as a kind of mental illness. (Richard Dawkins)

I do not concern myself with gods and spirits either good or evil nor do I serve any. (Lao Tzu)

Throw your dreams into space like a kite, and you do not know what it will bring back, a new life, a new friend, a new love, a new country. (Anais Nin)

The only authentic prayer is: Thy will be done. (Wilfred Shuchat, 1920-2018, Canadian scholar and rabbi)

Who sows virtue reaps honor. (Leonardo da Vinci)

Integrity means, more than honor, full integration of who you are: your modesty, compassion, gratitude, frugality especially--the "simplest gifts" in every religion and philosophy. *(I Ching)*

Character cannot be developed in ease and quiet. Only through experience of trial and suffering can the soul be strengthened, ambition inspired, and success achieved. (Helen Keller)

To know that you do not know is the best. To pretend to know when you do not know is disease. (Lao Tzu)

There are two kinds of truth: The truth that lights the way and the truth that warms the heart. The first of these is science and the second is art. (Raymond Chandler)

207

The quieter you become the more you can hear. (Ram Dass)

I'm a mystic. I believe in hearing the inaudible and touching the intangible and seeing the invisible. (Adam Clayton Powell Jr,)

I'm disappointed that success hasn't been a Himalayan feeling. (Gene Hackman)

Find ecstasy in life; the mere sense of living is joy enough. (Emily Dickenson)

I've taken up the *Bible* again, somewhat in the spirit of W. C. Fields--looking for loopholes. (David Niven)

Preach the Gospel at all times. When necessary, use words. (Saint Francis of Assisi)

Christianity isn't a failure; it just hasn't been tried yet. (G. K. Chesterton)

Be kind whenever possible. It is always possible. (Dalai Lama)

The greatest test of courage on the earth is to bear defeat without losing heart. (Robert Ingersoll)

Solitude is that human situation in which I keep myself company. (Hannah Arendt)

Have you ever found God in church? I never did. I just found a bunch of folks hoping for Him to show. Any God I ever felt in church I brought in with me. And I think all the other folks did too. They come to church to share God, not find God. (Alice Walker)

Being a Baptist won't keep you from sinning, but it'll sure as hell keep you from enjoying it. (Jimmy Dean)

It takes a man to suffer ignorance and smile. (Sting)

Manifest plainness, embrace simplicity, reduce selfishness, have few desires. (Lao Tzu)

Just when things look darkest, they go black. (Paul Newman)

Evil is relatively rare. Ignorance is epidemic. (Jon Stewart)

There's nothing wrong with shouting at God. (Robert Duvall)

Our prayers should be for blessings in general, for God knows best what is good for us. (Socrates)

If you don't fill your days with love, you are wasting your life. (James Broughton, 1913-1999, American poet and filmmaker)

Everyone thinks of God as a man. You can't help it. Santa Claus was a man, therefore God has to be a man. (Patti Smith)

I have lived to thank God that all my prayers have not been answered. (Jean Ingelow, 1820-1897, English poet and novelist)

Success is getting what you want. Happiness is wanting what you get. (Ingrid Bergman)

I prefer to think that God is not dead, just drunk. (John Huston)

I have always found that mercy bears richer fruits than strict justice. (Abraham Lincoln)

There's a crack in everything. That's how the light gets in. (Leonard Cohen)

Three things cannot be long hidden: The sun, the moon, and the truth. (Buddha)

Life is painting a picture, not doing a sum. (Oliver Wendell Holmes. Jr.)

Generosity gives assistance rather than advice. (Luc de Clapiers)

The fact is always obvious much too late, but the most singular difference between happiness and joy is that happiness is a solid and joy a liquid. (J. D. Salinger)

I urge you to please notice when you are happy, and exclaim or murmur or think at some point, "If this isn't nice, I don't know what is." (Kurt Vonnegut)

Love is supreme and unconditional; Like is nice but limited. (Duke Ellington)

It may be that we will have to repent in this generation. Not merely for the vitriolic words and the violent actions of the bad people, but for the appalling silence and indifference of the good people. (Martin Luther King, Jr.)

God and I have a great relationship, but we both see other people. (Dolly Parton)

I'll tell you one thing for sure: once you get to the point, where you're actually doing things for truth's sake, then nobody can ever touch you again because you're harmonizing with a greater power. (George Harrison)

Courage is resistance to fear, mastery of fear, not absence of fear. (Mark Twain)

The reward of suffering is experience. (Harry S. Truman)

We are not punished for our sins, but by them. (Elbert Hubbard,1856-1915, American writer, publisher, artist, and philosopher)

I'm not exactly a Buddhist Monk; I'm just old, which is almost the same thing. (Sparrow)

Honesty is the first chapter in the book of wisdom. (Thomas Jefferson)

If Satan wasn't around, churches would go out of business. (Marilyn Manson)

I don't think I've ever been an agnostic. I've always thought that there's a superior power, that this is not the real world and that there's a world to come. (Bob Dylan)

I do not believe in a fate that falls on men however they act, but I do believe in a fate that falls on them unless they act. (Buddha)

When miracles are admitted, every scientific explanation is out of the question. (Johannes Kepler)

God likes to give fancy slippers to people with one leg. (Irene Hennessy, Willy's Mom)

Obviously, you would give your life for your children, or give them the last biscuit on the plate. But to me, the trick in life is to take that sense of generosity between kin, make it apply to extended family and to your neighbor, your village and beyond. (Tom Stoppard)

211

Hatred corrodes the container it's carried in. (Alan Simpson, senator from Wyoming)

I refuse to accept the view that mankind is so tragically bound to the starless midnight of racism and war that the bright daybreak of peace and brotherhood can never become a reality. I believe that unarmed truth and unconditional love will have the final word. (Martin Luther King, Jr.)

What you are is God's gift to you; what you do with yourself is your gift to God. (Leo Buscaglia)

SPORTS

When I went to Catholic high school in Philadelphia, we just had one coach for football and basketball. He took all of us who turned out and had us run through a forest. The ones who ran into the trees were on the football team. (George Raveling)

The Supreme Court ruled that disabled golfer Casey Martin has a legal right to ride in a golf cart between shots at PGA Tour events. Man, the next thing you know, they're going to have some guy carry his clubs around for him. (Jon Stewart)

Every time a baseball player grabs his crotch, it makes him spit. That's why you should never date a baseball player. (Marsha Warfield, American actress and comedian)

It's good sportsmanship to not pick up lost golf balls while they are still rolling. (Mark Twain)

The only time my prayers are never answered is on the golf course. (Billy Graham)

My theme is, 'The spirit of friendship is the balance of life.' Not money. Not the World Series. It's friendship. The relationships I have with people, that's friendship. (Ernie Banks, Member of the Baseball Hall of Fame)

Skiing combines outdoor fun with knocking down trees with your face. (Dave Barry, American author and columnist)

Serious sport has nothing to do with fair play. It is bound up with hatred, jealousy, boastfulness, disregard of all rules and sadistic pleasure in witnessing violence. In other words, it is war minus the shooting. (George Orwell)

You are never too old to play chess! (Bobby Fischer)

There's no luck involved in chess. You just have to work at it. (Bobby Fischer)

Chess is a matter of delicate judgement, knowing when to punch and how to duck. (Bobby Fischer)

I never said most of the things I said. (Yogi Berra)

Nobody ever drowned in his own sweat. (Ann Landers)

All right everyone, line up alphabetically according to your height. (Casey Stengel)

Sports play a very important role in consolidating the national strength, adding lustre to the country's prestige and honor, inspiring people with national dignity and pride, and imbuing the whole society with revolutionary mettle. (Kim Jong-un)

Practice like you've never won. Play like you've never lost.

I know I am getting better at golf because I am hitting fewer spectators. (Gerald R. Ford)

I have two secret weapons...my legs, my arms and my brain. (Michael Vick)

All hockey players are bilingual. They know English and profanity. (Gordie Howe)

You prevent kids from joining gangs by offering after-school programs, sports, mentoring, and positive engagement with adults. You intervene with gang members by offering alternatives and employment to help redirect their lives. You deal with areas of high gang crime activity with real community policing. We know what works. (Greg Boyle, Homeboy Industries)

Thank you...fantasy football draft, for letting me know that even in my fantasies, I am bad at sports. (Jimmy Fallon)

Sports are a great place to show that equality can happen. (Venus Williams)

Personally, I rather look forward to a computer program winning the world chess championship. Humanity needs a lesson in humility. (Richard Dawkins)

There is a syndrome in sports called 'paralysis by analysis.' (Arthur Ashe)

Winning is not a sometime thing; it's an all-time thing. You don't win once in a while, you don't do things right once in a while, you do them right all the time. Winning is a habit. Unfortunately, so is losing. (Vince Lombardi)

GOR8RS (License plate)

Why did the golfer wear two pair of pants?...In case he got a hole in one.

The tennis ball doesn't know how old I am. The ball doesn't know if I'm a man or a woman or if I come from a communist country or not. Sport has always broken down these barriers. (Martina Navratilova)

I learned one thing from jumping motorcycles that was of great value on the golf course, the putting green especially: whatever you do, don't come up short. (Evel Knievel)

The uglier a man's legs are, the better he plays golf...it's almost a law. (H. G. Wells)

Thanksgiving dinners take eighteen hours to prepare. They are consumed in twelve minutes. Half-times take twelve minutes. This is not coincidence. (Erma Bombeck)

I consciously memorized the speed at which every pitcher in the league threw his fastball, curve and slider. Then, I'd pick up the speed of the ball in the first 30 feet of its flight and knew how it would move once it has crossed the plate. (Stan Musial)

Obviously a deer on the fairway has seen you tee off before and knows that the safest place to be when you play is right down the middle. (Jackie Gleason)

When you win, nothing hurts. (Joe Namath)

Competitive toughness is an acquired skill and not an inherited gift. (Chris Evert)

The Washington Bullets are changing their name. They don't want their team to be associated with crime. From now on, they'll just be known as the Bullets. (Jay Leno)

If you think golf is relaxing, you're not playing it right. (Bob Hope)

Me carrying a briefcase is like a hotdog wearing earrings. (Sparky Anderson, Major League Baseball player, coach and manager)

As they say in sports: the older you get, the better you used to be. (John McEnroe)

They throw the ball, I hit it. They hit the ball, I catch it. (Willie Mays)

THANK YOU

AFRIKAANS – ankie
ALBANIAN – faleminderit
ARABIC – shukran
ARMENIAN –chnorakaloutioun
BOSNIAN – hvala
BULGARIAN – благодаря / blagodaria
CANTONESE – M̀h'gōi
CROATIAN – hvala (HVAH-lah)
CZECH – děkuji (Dyekooyih)
DANISH – tak (tahg)
DUTCH – dank u
ENGLISH - thank you
ESTONIAN – tänan (TA-nahn)
FINNISH – kiitos (KEE-tohss)
FRENCH – merci
GERMAN – danke
GREEK – ευχαριστώ (ef-hah-rees-TOH)
HAWAIIAN – mahalo (ma-HA-lo)
HEBREW – תודה. / todah (toh-DAH)
HINDI – dhanyavād / shukriya
HUNGARIAN – köszönöm (KØ-sø-nøm)
ICELANDIC – takk (tahk)
INDONESIAN – terima kasih. (tuh-REE-mah KAH-see)
ITALIAN – grazie (GRAHT-tsyeh)
JAPANESE – arigatô (ah-ree-GAH-toh)
KOREAN – 감사합니다 (gamsahamnida)
LATVIAN – paldies (PUHL-dyehs)
LEBANESE – choukrane
LITHUANIAN – ačiū (AH-choo)
MACEDONIAN – Благодарам / blagodaram (blah-GOH-dah-rahm)
MALAY – terima kasih (TREE-muh KAH-seh)
MALTESE – grazzi (GRUTS-ee)
MANDARIN – Xièxiè
MONGOLIAN – Баярлалаа (bayarlalaa)

218

NORWEGIAN – takk
POLISH – dziękuję (Jenkoo-yen)
PORTUGUESE – obrigado [masculine] / obrigada [feminine]
ROMANIAN – mulţumesc (mool-tzoo-MESK)
RUSSIAN – спасибо (spuh-SEE-buh)
SERBIAN – хвала / hvala (HVAH-lah)
SLOVAK – Ďakujem (JAH-koo-yehm)
SLOVENIAN – hvala (HVAA-lah)
SPANISH – gracias (GRAH-syahs)
SWEDISH – tack
THAI – kop khun
TURKISH – teşekkür ederim (teh shek uer eh der eem)
UKRAINIAN – Дякую (DYAH-koo-yoo)
WELSH – diolch (DEE-ol'ch)
YIDDISH – a dank
ZULU – ngiyabonga

Knock. Knock.

Who's there?

Tank

Tank who?

You're welcome

VOCABULARY

ACADEME: An ancient school where morality and philosophy were taught.

ACADEMY: A modern school where football is taught. (Ambrose Bierce)

CARPE PER DIEM: Seize the check. (Robin Williams)

COFFEE: A person who is coughed upon.

EDIBLE: Good to eat and wholesome to digest, as a worm to a toad, a toad to a snake, a snake to a pig, a pig to a man, and a man to a worm. (Ambrose Bierce)

FUTURE: That period of time in which our affairs prosper, our friends are true and our happiness is assured. (Ambrose Bierce)

IRONY: The opposite of wrinkly.

KNICK-KNACK: A thing that sits on top of a what-not. (Oliver Hardy)

PHILOSOPHY: Reasoning why you are happy when you are poor.

PHOSPHORESCENCE: Now there's a word to lift your hat to…to find that phosphorescence, that light within, that's the genius behind poetry. (Emily Dickenson)

POLITICS: The shadow cast on society by big business. (John Dewey)

SABBATH: A weekly festival having its origin in the fact that God made the world in six days and was arrested on the seventh. (Ambrose Bierce)

TECHNOLOGY: The knack of so arranging the world that we don't have to experience it. (Max Frisch)

www.ingramcontent.com/pod-product-compliance
Lightning Source LLC
Chambersburg PA
CBHW051645260626
47170CB00004B/1339

* 9 7 8 0 5 7 8 4 9 0 8 5 4 *